Gaston's War

Vrijdag 17 Mei 1940.

4 u. 45 : einde alerte.

9 u. 30 : dejeuner : koffi

10.30

12.

14.

14.25

we moeten groote omweg
doen.

19.30 : Aussi le Chate
geen brood, geen dran
geen logement, niets

Gaston's War

A True Story of a Hero of the Resistance in World War II

Allan Mayer

★
Presidio

To all those men and women who sacrificed their lives for the freedom of their countries

Library of Congress Cataloging-in-Publication Data

Mayer, Allan J.
  Gaston's war.

  Bibliography: p. 204
  1. Vandermeerssche, Gaston.   2. World War,
1939–1945—Underground movements—Netherlands.
3. World War, 1939–1945—Personal narratives, Dutch.
4. Guerrillas—Netherlands—Biography.
I. Vandermeerssche, Gaston.   II. Title.
D802.N42V385   1988   940.53′ 492′0924   87–16890
ISBN 0-89141-291-3

Printed in the United States of America

Contents

Contents

Introduction

Though their origins were hazy, there had been Vandermeerssches living in the Flemish cathedral town of Ghent since the days of Napoleon. They were for the most part solid working folk who in the early part of the twentieth century had finally begun to make their way into the comfortable precincts of the middle class. In the years before World War I, Achilles Vandermeerssche built and ran Ghent's first mechanized carpentry-and-cabinetmaking shop. His son Joseph, a stern, authoritarian man who rejected the strict Catholicism of his ancestors, inherited the shop and made a good enough living from it for his family to afford both a house in the country and a cottage that they rented by the seashore for a month every year. But perhaps the most telling sign of the Vandermeerssche family's ascent up the socioeconomic ladder was the fact that Joseph's son Gaston had no plans to succeed his father in the shop. A student at the University of Ghent (the first of his family to get that far in school), he was determined to make his living with his head, not his hands.

Gaston Vandermeerssche was eighteen when the Germans invaded Belgium in the spring of 1940. He was a serious-minded young man, earnest and idealistic in the way that eighteen-year-olds who have not seen much of the world often are. For all that, he did not look the callow youth. Gaston had the opposite of a baby face; his was a long, narrow visage with a prominent nose and piercing eyes that his schoolmates insisted made him look three or four years older than he really was.

At the age of nine Gaston had applied for and won a prestigious and highly competitive educational grant from a fund organized to support gifted students. To keep the grant he had to finish each school year no less than third in his class. Since losing the grant would put an effective end to his education, he felt constantly pressured to perform, not just well, but brilliantly in school.

Gaston spent his days studying physics and mathematics at the university, his evenings and weekends tutoring less adept classmates, and whatever free time he had left working in his father's shop. He had little use for politics and even less for religion. (His faith was in science, he would tell anyone who asked, in the superiority of reason and logic.) He was, in short, conscientious, ambitious, and a tiny bit stuffy. Perhaps a bit brighter and more hardworking than most —and certainly more independent minded—but hardly remarkable.

As the "diary" that follows makes clear, however, this unremarkable young man went on to do some remarkable things. Within two years of the German invasion, he had become one of the most effective and important figures in the Allied underground—at the relatively tender age of twenty he was the architect, builder, and chief of an elaborate resistance network that employed more than fifteen hundred agents. In the end, the apolitical young physics student managed to become so painful a thorn in the side of the German occupation forces that when the Nazis finally caught him, they wound up condemning him to death no less than five separate times. Somehow, Gaston managed to survive—not simply the sentences, but two grim years of torture, beatings, and solitary confinement in a series of Gestapo prisons.

Gaston did not actually keep a daily record of his activities during the war. He tried at the very beginning, recognizing the enormous significance of what was happening and sensing somehow that one day he might be grateful to have a personal, contemporary account of what he had been through. The effort lasted all of seventeen days. There was simply too much going on and not enough time to get any of it down.

Not that it mattered in the end. Even if Gaston had forced himself to set aside the time a diary requires, he would have had to abandon the effort—for security reasons—when he joined the Belgian underground.

Thus, what follows is necessarily a reconstruction—the result of more than five years of research and interviews designed to reawaken and flesh out forty-year-old memories. The project began at the urging of Gaston's longtime friend Carl Moebius, who insisted that Gaston's mission as a freedom fighter would not be complete until he had told his story to a generation that (fortunately) has had little direct experience of war. With Moebius's help and encouragement, the effort quickly gathered steam. With his wife, Violette, and eighteen of their friends, Gaston revisited the principal sites of his wartime activities, including old safe houses, his route across the Pyrenees, and three of the former Gestapo prisons in which he had been held. He also sat down for more than one hundred hours of interviews—some conducted by the author, most by historian H. Carl Mueller.

If there is a particular point to recounting Gaston's wartime experiences forty years after the fact, it is to remind ourselves that individuals do not have to be victims, that even an inexperienced teenager can play a significant role in the great struggles of his time. These days, of course, it is easy to dismiss such notions as sentimental claptrap—ridiculously simplistic, not to mention hopelessly naive. Indeed, in a cynical age such as ours, it may be that one has to have lived a life like Gaston's to really believe that the individual can make a difference.

It was with this thought in mind that the idea of presenting Gaston's story in diary form occurred to the author—as a way of putting the reader into Gaston's shoes to the greatest extent possible, of allowing the reader to see the world through his eyes with not much more knowledge of, or perspective on, events than Gaston himself had at the time.

The hope, in other words, was that by use of a stylistic fiction a substantive truth could be revealed. If such turns out not to be the case, the blame should go entirely to the author, and not to the remarkable man whose story this is.

Allan Mayer

New York
December 1986

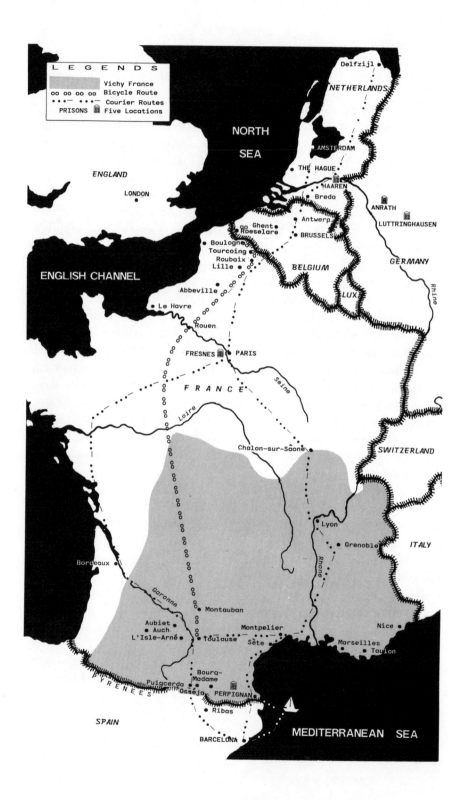

Chapter One

Odyssey to Nowhere

May 10, 1940. We are at war. How strange that seems, sitting in my quiet bedroom on this pleasant spring morning. The sun still shines as brightly as ever. The starlings continue to hunt for worms and insects in Mrs. Primo's garden next door. Yet men are dying— at least I think they are—almost within sight of my window.

It's just before 7:00 A.M. The house is silent. My parents and my sister are still asleep. When I first got up—about half an hour ago— everything seemed peaceful enough. As I tiptoed over to the marble-topped commode by the window, I could smell the tar-paper roof of Pa's cabinetmaking shop and the damp, freshly turned earth of Mrs. Primo's garden. I glanced out. Sure enough, there she was, already at work with her spade.

I figured I'd shave (not that I really need to every day, but I think it's a habit worth getting into) and then go down to the kitchen. I had just started, using the old straightedge razor that Pa gave me last summer when I turned eighteen.

Suddenly, a shriek from outside shattered the early-morning silence. My hand jerked, and the white lather on my chin began to turn a bright red. Cursing under my breath, I pressed a towel to the cut and looked out the window.

Mrs. Primo was standing in the middle of her garden, pointing up at the sky, wailing her head off. "My God! My God!" she was crying. "The Germans are coming! The Germans are coming!"

In the distance, high above the outskirts of the city, I could see black puffs of smoke smudging the bright-blue sky—flak from our antiaircraft batteries. Listening hard, I could just make out the drone of German fighter planes. They seemed to be bypassing Ghent, heading west toward the coast.

Still holding the towel to my chin, I went to the table by my bed and turned on my crystal radio set. At first, all I got was static. In the garden below, Mrs. Primo was shouting something about German bombers. Finally, I managed to tune in a clear signal. "Early this morning the German Wehrmacht attacked Holland and Belgium," a solemn voice intoned. "The Belgian government has announced that Belgium is in a state of war. All Belgian army units are being mobilized. All regular and reserve personnel are to report to their units immediately."

The signal faded.

That was ten minutes ago. Since then I've been sitting on my bed, wondering if I should wake my parents. I don't think I will— there's no immediate danger. They'll hear the bad news soon enough.

I get up and walk back to the commode to inspect my chin in the mirror. I can't help but smile. The war's hardly begun, and already I'm wounded.

Half an hour later I'm dressed and downstairs, sitting quietly at the big wooden table in my mother's spotless kitchen, chewing on a piece of bread, wondering what the day will bring.

I can't believe the Germans have really invaded. What happened to our neutrality? All those measures we took (or didn't take), such as not building defensive fortifications along the German border, or not continuing the Maginot Line, or refusing to sign any military treaties with the English or the French—wasn't all that enough for the Germans? And what about all those debates at the university in which everyone agreed that our neutrality would protect us—could everyone have been so wrong?

I remember all those horror stories Pa used to tell me about the 1914–18 war with Germany, those four terrible years he spent in the trenches and bunkers along the coast. Was all that for nothing?

All that suffering, all those sacrifices—weren't they supposed to bring an end to war once and for all? And yet, here we are, just twenty years later, and those same Germans are attacking us once again, without reason, without respect for our neutrality.

It's just unbelievable. Here I am, on the brink of what should be the most important period in my life. I've been working so hard. I can't remember taking a single day off in . . . what? Six or seven years, at least. As soon as vacation begins, Pa puts me to work in the shop. And during the school year, what with money being so short and all, I've been spending practically more time tutoring other students than studying for my own courses.

This was the year I was going to lay the groundwork for my career. This was the year I was going to sign up for two majors, mathematics *and* physics. I know it's risky, but I've taken risks before. It'll just take a little extra effort. And then one day I'll be able to look back with pride . . . one day when I'm a professor myself.

But what happens now? Am I going to get dragged into a war for four years like my father was? Maybe it will last even longer. Maybe I'll be wounded or crippled—or even killed. God, all those discussions with my classmates about the fear of death. "I'm not afraid of death," I would tell them. "Even if you told me that I am going to die right now, it wouldn't make any difference to me."

What is going to happen? There are so many unknowns. That doesn't frighten me. If anything, I think the idea of "unknowns" excites me. It's a challenge, isn't it?

But what about the family? Will Pa have to go back into the army? He must be too old. But who knows? Knowing his hatred for the Germans, he might just volunteer. And my mother—what will it do to her? She doesn't complain, but I know her health isn't very good. I can hear her gasping for breath each time she goes up the stairs to do the beds.

There is a noise at the front of the house. It's Mrs. Primo, pounding at the door, shouting about the Germans. I rush over to quiet her before she wakes up everyone, but it's too late. My mother is already coming down the stairs.

She opens the door, and Mrs. Primo stumbles in, tears streaming down her cheeks. She's Italian and has relatives living under the Fascist dictatorship in Rome. "The Germans will overrun us, just like they did Denmark and Norway," she sobs. "They'll make us their slaves. All the men and boys will be taken to labor camps." She collapses into a chair and buries her face in her apron.

I can't believe she's talking this way. Why are women always so hysterical? "What's the matter with you?" I bark at her, a little surprised at how angry she makes me. "You think we're just going to roll over and play dead? Between our own defense forces and the French and British armies, we're going to give the Germans a fight they won't forget."

Mrs. Primo blinks in surprise, then looks up at my mother and starts crying even harder. "He's just like the other young men," she wails. "They never believe they'll be killed."

I start to answer, but my mother gives me an angry look. Mrs. Primo lost her father and brother in the last war. I decide it's time to leave for school.

The Gothic buildings of the University of Ghent cluster atop a hill overlooking the Lye River. I can usually walk there in twenty minutes. Today it takes me just ten. Breathless, I arrive to find knots of students crowding the wide marble steps of the science building, exchanging rumors, speculating about the future. Everyone's desperate for news.

The leftists are already organizing a resistance. My old pal Frans says he won't speak to me anymore if I don't join.

Not everyone's preparing to fight. Fat Georges, the bully who always used to play the elephant when we acted out Kipling stories as kids, is standing in the middle of one group of students, holding forth on how the Germans are our friends. According to him, the British and French are being manipulated by Jews and Communists. "They're weak and corrupt," he says. "They're not ready to fight."

"And *you* are?" I ask him, unable to resist. "You couldn't even run up the stairs to your next class."

"I won't have to fight when the Germans get here," he replies. "I'll be happy to see them. And you, my friend, you'll be happy to know me." He smiles at me in his smarmy way. "Remember, Gaston, you are Flemish—not Walloon or French."

"I know what I am," I snap, and walk off.

If only things were as simple as people like Georges try to make them seem. We speak Flemish at home, my parents and sister and

I. (Simone also speaks fairly good French, which makes me jealous—it's not right that my sister can do something I can't.) At school, of course, children aren't supposed to speak Flemish, but rather Dutch, the "official" language of radio, newspapers, and so forth. Myself, I don't mind. I like Dutch—so much so that I even became president of a group that promotes its use. Speaking Dutch seems to me to be more intellectual than speaking Flemish. What's more, it brings you into a wider world. After all, Dutch isn't only an official language of Belgium, it's what they speak in the Netherlands.

The trouble is, a lot of people think speaking Dutch is snobbish. Even worse, it has pro-German political connotations. During the 1914–18 war, the Flemish collaborators who worked with the Germans generally spoke Dutch. That's why Pa got so mad when I started using Dutch at home. "We are not collaborators here!" he shouted at me.

Well, I've got no love for the Germans, that's for sure. (Though I must admit, there are some Nazi sympathizers in our language club.) It bothers me that my feelings about the language make Pa distrust my political sympathies. I wish we could discuss it openly. I wish we could discuss anything openly. Verbal communication with Pa is generally limited to him answering "yes" or "no" (mostly "no") to hesitant requests of mine that I usually try out on Mother beforehand.

I can talk to Mother. She understands my feelings about the Dutch-Flemish question (and says I should "not insist" with Pa). The fact is, there is no question that the Flemish have been oppressed by the Walloons. In the army, for example, almost all the officers are Walloons; a Flemish boy doesn't have a chance. This is unfair. When a high government official or a member of the royal family speaks to the nation, it is always in French, never in Flemish. It's as if we Flemish don't exist. Most of the economic development in heavy industry has been in the Walloon side of Belgium—in Flanders industry is dying. That's not right. We deserve to be treated the same as the Walloons.

I feel strongly about that. In fact, until the Germans attacked, I was ready to fight if that was what it took to ensure that we got what we deserved. But now, with our nation under attack, we should pull together, not give in to this stupid internal squabble. Flemish or Walloon, we are still all Belgians. Citizens of a free, sovereign, and, above all, *neutral* nation. The Germans had no right to attack us.

For the most part, I keep my feelings to myself. They say German sympathizers are already drawing up lists of those who oppose them. I'm not worried about Georges, but I am worried about some of his silent friends. As Pa says, "Watch out for the ones who are listening, not the ones who are talking."

Professor De Bruyne is lecturing on the theories of Max Planck this morning. I love physics, but I can't concentrate—not today. How can we hide in lecture halls discussing theory and philosophy while bombs are dropping all around us?

I find myself thinking about a book I read the other day. It told the story of Edith Cavell, a British nurse who served in Belgium during the last war. "La Dame Blanche," they called her. She not only tended the sick, she also gathered intelligence and helped prisoners of war escape from the Germans. In the end, she was betrayed and shot.

Why, I ask myself, did Cavell risk her life like that? It couldn't have been blind patriotism. After all, she was in a foreign country, helping mainly foreigners. Then again, perhaps she was responding to a wider, higher kind of patriotism—a patriotism that reaches farther than the borders of one's own nation. Perhaps there is a patriotism that relates to *people* regardless of their nationality, a patriotism that recognizes that anything that divides people is bad, a patriotism that understands that freedom must be defended whenever and wherever it is threatened.

Who knows? What counts right now is that we've been invaded. Our soldiers are fighting the Wehrmacht. Our cities are being bombed by the Luftwaffe. Our people are dying. Perhaps before today we could afford to argue about politics. But now our freedom is at stake. We're at war, and for the second time in twenty years the Germans are our enemy.

May 11, 1940. Up early. The radio is broadcasting conflicting reports. Some say the Germans are breaking through our lines. Others claim they've been pushed back. There's talk that all men over the age of sixteen will soon be ordered to report for military service.

I head for the main railroad station, the most likely place for mobilization orders and other news to be posted.

The streets are crowded with men—some in uniform, most wearing only part of a uniform (and an old, ill-fitting part at that). There's a large crowd at the station. Plenty of rumors, but no hard news. I hear one man say that the army has commandeered all the trains; another says that the Germans are bombing the tracks along the coast. There's nothing to do but go back home.

In the evening the radio reports that Eben Emael—a major fort near the border—is under siege. Our men have been ordered not to surrender but to fight to the death.

May 12, 1940. The news is bad. The radio reports heavy losses at the front. We're blowing up the major canal and river crossings in an effort to slow down the invading Panzer divisions. But the Germans simply throw down pontoon bridges and keep advancing.

Fears are growing that we'll soon be overrun. The roads are beginning to fill with cars and trucks loaded down with people and their belongings.

May 13, 1940. I wake at dawn to hear King Leopold III on the radio. "For the second time in a quarter of a century," he says, "Belgium, loyal and neutral, is being attacked by the Germans. Faced with the choice between sacrifice and disgrace, the Belgium of 1940 does not hesitate any more than the one of 1914."

The king pauses. Had he been speaking to a crowd rather than to a radio microphone, I'm sure a cheer would have gone up. "France and England," he continues, "have promised their help. Like my father in 1914, I will head our army—with the same faith and with the same conscience. Belgium's cause is pure. With God's help she will triumph."

The king is followed by an announcer who reads a proclamation ordering all ablebodied men between the ages of sixteen and thirty-five to report for army duty. The men of east Flanders are to go to Roeselare, near the French border. That's just seventy kilometers west of here. I can ride there in a few hours on Pa's bicycle.

May 14, 1940. I spend the day packing and repacking my small bag. I want to take as little as possible. In the end, I settle on one change of clothes, Pa's old razor, a small notebook, my toothbrush, and a map.

May 15, 1940. I'm up and ready to go by 7:00 A.M. Trouble is, I can't leave without saying good-bye to Pa, and he doesn't come down to breakfast until nearly eight. When he finally appears, he looks me over and shakes his head. "I suppose you must go and do your duty," he says, frowning. "I hope the war is over before you see any action." He gives me the addresses of some people he knows and trusts who live in the west.

My mother tries to act cheerful, but I can see the fear in her eyes. "Don't worry," I tell her. "I'll be back before you know I'm gone."

I wheel the bicycle out of the house. My parents and sister stand in the doorway, as if seeing me off on a camping trip.

My first stop is my friend Arnold's house. We've spent many hours studying math together. Perhaps we can keep up our studies on the road.

When I get there, I find him still in his pajamas. "Aren't you coming?" I ask.

"The war's almost over," he shrugs. "What's the point?"

I stare at him. How can he be so casual? Doesn't he realize what's at stake here? I recall Pa telling me about the traitors who helped the Germans during the last war—how they didn't seem to care what happened to Belgium. Pa despised such people from the bottom of his heart.

But Arnold? How could he be a traitor?

I climb back on my bike and ride off. If I have to go by myself, I'll go by myself.

The road to Roeselare is choked with people—some clinging to the running boards of cars and trucks, others on bicycles, many on foot. An endless stream of refugees is moving in both directions, dragging with them overloaded carts and wagons filled with everything they own. A woman wearing a heavy coat and her Sunday hat pushes a baby carriage containing a large grandfather clock. Another carries a squalling baby next to a cart filled with crates of cackling chickens.

The day is warm and sunny. The farmers stand in their fields, watching the chaos on the road.

It's late in the afternoon when I finally get to Roeselare. There's a huge crowd gathered outside the train station. I ask a group of boys sitting on their knapsacks what's going on. They tell me there's been a change of plans. Now we're supposed to report to Ieper, another twenty or so kilometers to the west. With a sigh, I get back on my bicycle.

Just west of Roeselare I meet the war head on. A large black automobile is lying in a ditch, perforated with bullet holes. Nearby, a teenage boy and his father kneel over a blood-spattered woman, frantically tearing strips of cloth from the bottom of her dress in an effort to bind her wounds.

My knees go weak, and I look away. Across the road, an old man— a farmer or laborer, from the look of his clothing—is sitting on the ground, his back propped up against a tree, holding a bloodstained handkerchief to his leg. "It was a Stuka," he says. "Came screaming out of the sky like the devil. Shot up the road for a quarter mile."

I remember my first-aid training and look at his wound. It doesn't seem serious, and I run back across the road to ask for bandages. The teenage boy is crying in his father's arms. The blood-spattered woman—his mother—is dead.

The road ahead is even more crowded with refugees—confused, tired, frightened. The villagers along the way are normally hospitable to strangers; now they are becoming overwhelmed.

It's nearly dark by the time I get to Ieper. One of the addresses Pa gave me was that of an old army friend of his from the last war, a man whom he described as a good patriot and a great soldier. The man's name is De Smul, and he lives in a large house surrounded by a low wrought-iron fence with blossoming fruit trees in the front garden. Hoping he'll offer me a place to stay for the night, I park my bike at the gate, walk up the brick path, and ring the bell.

The door is opened by a beautiful blonde girl wearing thick red lipstick. She takes my breath away. None of the girls I know wear makeup like that. Stammering, I tell her who I am. She introduces herself as De Smul's daughter and leads me into a book-lined study. Mr. De Smul is sitting by the window, smoking a pipe and watching the sky. "The British Spitfires have been chasing the German Stukas all afternoon," he says, "but it seems the show is over."

De Smul has the bearing of a military man, with thick white hair combed straight back. He remembers my father fondly. When they fought together, they weren't much older than I am now. "There is a terrible beauty about the noise and excitement of war," he tells me. Nonetheless, he is not eager to see another one. "Only the victor speaks of war as a game and describes the warriors as heroes," he says. "You must not think of the heroes, but of the innocent people who suffer and die."

I go to bed right after dinner. The constant wail of air-raid sirens makes it difficult to sleep. I dream fitfully—of the dead woman on the road, of surging crowds of refugees being driven off a cliff by screaming dive-bombers, of a pretty girl with red lipstick smiling at me across a dinner table.

May 16, 1940. A hearty breakfast with De Smul and his daughter, then back on my bike. I ride to the railroad station, where once again I find a large crowd of confused would-be soldiers. Posters and announcements over the station loudspeakers warn us to watch what we say about troop movements. There may be secret agents and saboteurs in our midst. I have to laugh. How can we betray any secrets when we don't know where we're going ourselves?

Suddenly, I spot a familiar face in the crowd. It's Max, one of my best friends from school, looking as lost and confused as everyone else. He too has bicycled from Ghent hoping to get a chance to fight for his country. God, I'm glad to see him. Max is okay. His father, who managed a garage, died a few years ago. Though he's no older than me, Max immediately took over his father's job, assuming the role of breadwinner for his mother. He's got a kind of precocious maturity that I can sympathize with.

Max is just as happy to see me as I am to see him, and we decide to stick together. A few minutes later we hear an announcement that the Belgian army recruiting center has been moved to Rouen. That's way on the other side of the French border, a good 250 kilometers southwest of here. And no trains are expected for at least another day.

How can things be so disorganized?

In the end, Max and I decide to see if we can find any more friends from Ghent and make our own train—with our bicycles.

Within a few minutes we've rounded up five schoolmates: Marcel, a good-natured show-off from a wealthy family; tubby Lou, with his sweaty handshake and greasy hair; and the three Bouvet brothers, Paul, Frans, and Josef. Like Max and me, Marcel and Lou rode here on their bicycles. But the Bouvets hitchhiked down from Ghent— meaning we are seven people with only four bikes.

Max suggests that we double up. Since he is small, he takes Josef, the youngest of the Bouvets. Marcel gets Paul, and Lou gets Frans. Because my bike has two luggage carriers (one attached to the handlebars, the other slung over the rear wheel), I'm selected to be the baggage car of our little train.

We push off under a bright sun. I weave about crazily, trying to balance the heavy load of luggage strapped to my bike. The road is choked with traffic. The noise of automobile horns and shouting people is deafening. Thunder rumbles in the distance. Some peasants are driving heavy farm wagons loaded down with their belongings. Most people, however, are on foot, carrying what they can on their backs. The spring wheat is ripening in the fields on either side of the road, but no one pays it any mind.

I stop to help an old woman who has dropped her bundle. There is anguish and terror in her face. I look away, staring at a field of yellow mustard plants rippling in the breeze. It's hard to believe that the thunder in the distance is the sound of bombs falling, of people dying.

We reach the French border at Leseau just after noon. The line of refugees seems endless. It takes several hours before we are allowed across. Our goal for the day is the village of Bethune, about thirty kilometers southwest of the frontier. It's late in the afternoon, and we are nearly there when a gendarme appears on the road and flags us down.

The village, he says, is off limits. The Germans bombed it last night, and we could be shot for looters. Though exhausted, we have no choice but to continue on. The youngest of the Bouvets starts to cry. I can't really blame him.

We ride another twenty kilometers, reaching the village of Bruay-en-Artois just as the sun goes down. There's a large stone fountain in the village square. We lean our bicycles against it and soak our sore feet in the cool water. Three local girls—sisters, by the look of them—stroll by and start laughing at us. "Don't you know it's against the law to wash your feet in the fountain?" the eldest shouts at us in French. "If you don't stop, we'll call the gendarmes on you."

Marcel (the only fluent speaker of French in our group) responds by jumping into the fountain and splashing water at them. "Go ahead— call the gendarmes," he yells back. "They won't arrest us. We're on our way to join the Belgian army. We're going to save you from the Germans."

This makes the girls laugh even harder. I suggest to Marcel that he ask them if they can help us find some food and a place to stay for the night.

He does, and the eldest girl—who introduces herself as Gisele— agrees to take us home to meet her father. She leads us to a large house just off the square with a courtyard surrounded by high stone walls. An old man is sitting on a chair in the courtyard, reading a newspaper.

"Papa, look!" Gisele calls to him. "We've found some war heroes!"

The old man stands up and looks us over. "I was a captain in the army in the last war," he says. "My home is yours."

We're taken inside into a large kitchen, where we all sit down to a supper of early spring greens, potatoes, eggs, and wine. We're so hungry we wolf down our food without a word. Gisele's father doesn't seem to mind. He's more than happy to do all the talking himself.

The war is going badly, he tells us. The French were too confident that the Maginot Line could never be breached. "Perhaps we were blinded by the hope that we'd never see the terrible madness of war again," he says. He asks us if we're willing to die for our country, to give up our lives so that others may live in freedom. "Are you willing to kill another human being?" he shouts. "When the bullets are flying and you see the enemy in front of you, will you be able to pull the trigger?" He doesn't mean to frighten us, he says, but these are the sorts of questions we're going to have to face in the days ahead.

After the plates are cleared, Gisele invites me to go for a walk. The night is clear and filled with stars. I can stare up at them for hours. They make some people feel small and insignificant. But they fill me with a sense of peace and calm. I feel secure because I know they'll always be there.

I have no trouble finding my favorite constellation, Ursa Major. I point it out to Gisele. If you know the sky, I tell her, you'll never be lost.

She takes my hand and smiles at me. I feel awkward. All of a sudden, it hits me how terribly inexperienced I am when it comes to girls. Here I am talking of stars to someone who clearly doesn't know anything about them and probably cares even less. What do you say to a girl you've just met and probably will never see again?

Most of the girls I've known were friends of my sister. I'd look them over when they came by to visit Simone. Most of them were skinny little things. Not Gisele. I can't keep from stealing glances at her body. She's got an amazing figure, much better developed than that of any of Simone's friends. God, I'm blushing furiously. I try to look at her without her noticing, but she catches my eye. That makes me blush even more.

I feel terrible. I have no idea what to say to her. Why did she choose me for a walk? Was it because of my old face? How awful.

Eventually, I suggest that we go back inside. It's perfect weather for the Luftwaffe.

May 17, 1940. A bad night. German bombers keep us up until just before dawn. After a breakfast of French bread and strong black coffee, Gisele's father urges us on our way. "The Germans are coming very fast," he says. "The army will need every one of you."

Once again traffic on the main road is very heavy. We pedal steadily until just after noon, when we reach the village of St. Pol, twenty-five kilometers southwest of Bruay. On the outskirts of the village, we stop under some trees and decide to have a picnic.

We are ravenous and gobble down all the wine and cheese Gisele's father gave us. Then we all fall asleep in the warm sun.

I dream of something that happened on a similar spring day, many years past, back in Ghent. I'm about seven and am playing in the attic with my sister, Simone. She helps me open the skylight, and I crawl out onto the tile roof of our house. I am very high up, but I feel no fear, only excitement. There is a patch of moss on the

tiles with some small flowers growing from it. I reach for them.
Suddenly, I hear church bells ringing. Someone is shouting my name.
It's one of our neighbors. She's shrieking that I'm going to fall. I
turn and start to lose my footing on the wet tiles . . .

I open my eyes, my heart pounding. Marcel is yelling at me to
wake up. The Germans are bombing St. Pol. As we watch, a bomb
hits the village church. The tall steeple teeters for a moment, then
topples over.

People are screaming and shouting, fleeing their homes. There is
smoke and fire everywhere.

Lou begins to cry. He wants to go home. Max says there's no
turning back.

A Frenchman rides by on a bicycle, shouting at us to stay off the
main road. The Germans are bombing everything in sight.

We pedal furiously down the bumpy rural lanes, reaching Doullens,
a good-sized town some thirty kilometers to the south, late in the
afternoon. It's been completely evacuated. The roads here are nearly
impassable, pocked with bomb craters and crowded with refugees.
We have nothing to eat or drink, nowhere to go. Hungry and tired,
we decide to head back to St. Pol.

It's dark by the time we get there. Unable to find a place to
stay, we push on to the next village. At the outskirts we're stopped
by a French soldier, who points his rifle at us and demands that
we identify ourselves. We explain that we're trying to reach the
Belgian army recruiting center in Rouen. He tells us we can't stay
here—we must keep moving. "There'll be troops coming through
tomorrow," he says. "The Germans will be bombing the road and
the village."

For Paul, this is the last straw. "This is stupid!" he shouts. "The
Germans are everywhere! By the time we get to Rouen, they'll probably have overrun all of Belgium. We might as well go home."

Marcel shakes his head in disgust and calls Paul a Nazi coward.
With an incoherent cry, Paul leaps on him. The two tumble to the
ground, rolling in the dirt, kicking and punching each other. Max
and I have to pull them apart.

Eventually, we all get back on our bikes and find a small road
that goes around the village. Shortly after midnight, we stop and
make camp in a field of tall grass, too tired to go any further. The

ground is cold and wet with dew, and we huddle together for warmth. I feel very alone, lost in a strange country, not even sure where it is I am trying to go.

May 18, 1940. We are up with the first rays of the sun, shivering in the morning cold. There is nothing to eat or drink, so we get on our bikes and push off. The countryside here is very hilly, and we're forced to walk our bikes as much as we ride them.

We take turns running to farmhouses to beg for food. Unfortunately, the local people's hospitality has long since been exhausted by the thousands of refugees who have been streaming through here for the past few days.

Around noon, near the village of Gancourt, a farmer lets us wash ourselves off in his horse trough. We ask for food, but he has none to give.

Beyond Gancourt, the road is so full of ruts we cannot ride at all. We're heading for Abbeville, near the mouth of the Somme, about one hundred kilometers northeast of our ultimate destination, Rouen. After walking for two hours, we're stopped by a gendarme, who asks where we're going. We explain about the Belgian army recruiting center in Rouen and tell him we haven't had anything to eat or drink in two days.

He is sympathetic but firm. We cannot enter Abbeville. The Germans have just bombed it. Wearily, we make our way around the village. The road is slightly better here, so we get back on our bikes. Barely a kilometer later, Marcel's bike hits a rut, throwing him and Paul to the ground.

They aren't hurt, but the bike's rear tire is punctured and its chain is broken. Max surveys the damage and shakes his head. There's nothing he can do without tools. "We'll have to walk to a farm and ask for help," he says.

I walk alongside Marcel. He's dizzy from lack of food and not sure how much longer he can go on. I tell him to concentrate on getting over the next hill. That's all he should think about—not how hungry he is, not how bad he feels, just getting over that next hill.

After another hour or so of walking, we reach a large, prosperous-looking farm. The farmer has no food to spare, but he does lend Max the tools he needs to fix Marcel's bike.

After Max finishes patching the flat, he sends Marcel off to get a
bucket of water so he can test the tire for leaks. A few minutes
later Marcel returns with two liters of wine.

Max rolls his eyes. "I asked for water, not wine," he says. "I
can't use wine to fix a flat."

"Why not?" Marcel replies. "It's a liquid, isn't it? You can use it
to check for leaks, and then we can drink it."

That's just what we do. It tastes delicious.

Three hours later we arrive in Airaines. It seems untouched by the
war. As we walk our bikes through the village, we pass an old woman
working in a garden in front of a stone cottage. In broken French,
Max explains who we are and that we haven't eaten in more than
two days.

She looks us over, then invites us inside.

The old woman's kitchen is warm and smells of spices and freshly
baked bread. She gives us cheese and bread and apples, all she
has. "The more you eat," she says, "the less there will be for the
Germans."

We push on. By dusk we've reached the banks of the Somme, near
Ailly. There's a large farm at a fork in the road. We ride our bikes
into the courtyard and are immediately surrounded by a gang of
small children and several barking dogs.

A moment later the owner of the farm rides up on a black horse.
He's a tall, aristocratic man with a bushy mustache, and he immediately offers us food and shelter.

We're just starting for the kitchen when there are shouts from
the nearby fields. The farmhands are pointing to the horizon—where
we see a huge formation of planes heading straight toward us.

We all start running for the storm cellar, then stop. The planes
aren't German Stukas, but British Spitfires! We cheer as they roar
by.

May 19, 1940. Sunday. We sleep (in real beds!) until past 10:00
A.M., when the farmer and his family return from church. After a
breakfast of cider, fresh bread, and jam, we continue on our way.

It's sunny and clear—perfect weather for the Luftwaffe. Though
it makes for harder going, we stick to small side roads. In the distance

we can see villages being bombed. We see the flames and smoke long before we actually hear the explosions.

By late afternoon we reach Blangy. A small boy with a dog takes us home to his father, who agrees to let us sleep in his barn—and eat all the eggs we can find!

May 20, 1940. Awakened by the wail of air-raid sirens. Then explosions—close enough to shake us out of our straw beds.

We rush outside. Stukas are dive-bombing the village. Several houses are in flames.

We jump on our bikes and head for the main road south, just ahead of a small crowd of refugees, most of them on foot.

Suddenly we hear shouting and screaming behind us. Two Messerschmitts are diving at the road, guns blazing.

We hurl ourselves into a ditch. The Germans strafe the road twice, then fly off.

Cautiously, we crawl back onto the road. Two men and a woman are lying on the pavement next to a cart, literally shot to pieces. A little girl is sprawled on top of the cart. She too is dead. In all we count twelve bodies.

The German planes are still strafing the road up ahead. We hide in a small grove of trees, waiting for them to stop.

The shooting and bombing go on for nearly four hours. Finally, just after noon, we start for Neufchatel.

We ride all afternoon under an intense sun without seeing a single house. At dusk we are again forced to jump in a ditch when Max spots four more German planes coming in low over the fields.

Finally, near Neufchatel, we find an old, abandoned barn. We push our way through a thicket of cobwebs and use a tree branch to sweep out a clear area in which we can sleep.

May 21, 1940. Up at dawn, cold and hungry. We push off, hoping to make Rouen by nightfall. The land here is less cultivated, with small forests and many hills. Tall sycamore trees line the road, their branches forming high arches that shield us from both the sun and the Luftwaffe.

As a result, our progress is swift, and we reach Rouen late in the afternoon. Marcel plays tour guide as we pedal down a cobblestone street that runs along the Seine. "Joan of Arc was burned at the stake here in 1431," he tells us.

In front of Notre Dame Cathedral, we meet a soldier who helps us find a place to stay.

May 22, 1940. It's been exactly a week since I left Ghent. So far I've ridden nearly three hundred kilometers.

It feels as if I've been on the road for months. I wish there were some way to communicate with my parents. I am very worried. Are they still at home in Ghent? Did my father leave to fight the Germans? What has happened to his business? If the Germans occupy the city, will they conscript him to work for them as they did his father? I know Pa would refuse to do any work for the Germans— just as my grandfather refused. How much I admire him for what he did in the 1914–18 war. I'm sorry I never once even tried to tell him how I feel about him.

The news we are hearing isn't very good. The Germans are moving up very fast. They call it a "blitzkrieg." Holland has already been overrun and has surrendered.

I wonder how they will train us fast enough to join in the fighting.

In the morning we walk to the Belgian consulate. An attaché checks our identity papers and tells us to report to the army barracks on the Avenue General Leclerc.

A crowd of several hundred men is standing outside the barracks. The mood is grim. The Germans, we are told, have overrun Amiens and Arras. The French have lost fifteen divisions in ten days.

Inside we show our papers to a corporal, who tells us that the Belgian recruiting center has been moved south to Toulouse. That's all the way on the other side of France, nearly 750 kilometers from here! It might as well be on the moon.

At least we're not expected to bicycle there. There'll be a train, we're told—though just when no one knows.

We wait all day under a hot sun on the parade ground in front of the barracks. No train. Paul doesn't think it will ever come.

May 23, 1940. Another day waiting at the parade ground. Rumors are spreading that no trains are moving anywhere. There's also talk that the French and British armies are in retreat.

May 24, 1940. After breakfast Max suggests that the seven of us try to make it to Toulouse on our own. The Bouvets are less than enthusiastic about the idea, but we eventually manage to convince them that it's better than sitting around on our bottoms.

We bicycle off just before noon. The sun is very hot, and the hills are higher and steeper than any we have experienced. We spend much of the time walking our bicycles.

After a few hours Paul starts to complain. "It was a mistake to leave Rouen," he says. "At least there we had a place to eat and sleep." I tell him to stop grumbling. The decision to leave was made jointly, and we owe it to each other to make the best of it.

Around 7:00 P.M. we reach Bernay, a small town fifty or so kilometers southeast of Rouen. A group of young girls gives us a big hello, but we cannot find a place to stay.

We push on. Several hours later, in the middle of nowhere, we find a deserted barn. Too tired to go any further, we walk our bicycles inside.

Three men are sleeping in the hayloft. They shout at us to go away.

"Go away yourself!" Paul shouts back.

The three men jump down from the loft. They're a few years older than us and pretty disreputable looking to boot. "You can leave on your own two feet, or we can throw you out," one of them says.

Without any warning, Paul lashes out and punches the man in the face. Suddenly, we're all fighting. It's crazy. Europe is in flames, and here we are brawling in a barn. How can people be so petty?

Finally, Max and I manage to restore some order. We agree that the three men can have the hayloft. The seven of us will sleep on the barn floor.

May 25, 1940. We're up by 6:30 A.M. and leave without seeing our barn-mates in the loft. Around 8:30 we reach Sees, some 130 kilometers southeast of Rouen. Pigs would be received better than we are. No one will help us or give us food.

We push on to Alençon, a good-sized town. On the way, we buy some bread and wine—for five times what we paid a few days ago.

Early in the evening we arrive in Parennes, a small village seven kilometers south of Alençon. Frans Bouvet volunteers to watch the bikes while the rest of us go off in search of food.

We return empty-handed to find that Frans has drunk all our wine. "I'm not sleeping in a field or a barn tonight," he announces. "I'm going to find the mayor of this town and get him to give us a good place to stay."

With that, he wanders off. A few minutes later he's back. To our amazement, he has a slip of paper with a name and an address on it. "The mayor says these people have three sons in the war," he reports, "so they should have room for us."

The house is on the outskirts of the village. We knock on the door and are greeted by a beautiful teenage girl with thick red hair and pale-blue eyes. "I am Paulette Blondeau," she says, flashing a dazzling smile. "You must be friends of my brothers." Marcel explains that we're not, though we could be. Paulette laughs and leads us into the kitchen. Then she goes to fetch her parents.

As soon as she leaves, Marcel lets out a long, low whistle. "God," he says, "if she smiles at me like that once more . . ." He shakes his head.

Paulette's parents give us dinner, then offer us the use of their sons' rooms. Even if we double up, two to a bed, one of us will still have to sleep on the living-room sofa. To prevent any more arguments, I volunteer.

May 26, 1940. I awake to the smell of hot chocolate. It's Sunday, and the Blondeaus are getting ready for church.

Paulette invites me to come with them. I decline. I've never been able to understand how otherwise sensible people can be taken in by the mumbo jumbo of organized religion. I agree with my father: over the centuries, the Church has been responsible for a lot more harm than good. I'll take empirical observation and the scientific method over superstitious faith any day.

In the afternoon we all wash our clothes in a large concrete trough just outside the kitchen door. Paulette stands next to me, her sleeves rolled up, laughing as Max and Marcel tease each other. Her thick copper hair is piled high on her head, held in place by a large clasp. A single stray wisp curls down her long, slender neck. Her cheeks are flushed, and her large eyes sparkle. I've never seen anything so beautiful.

Catching me staring, Paulette flashes a wicked grin and splashes some water at me. I splash back. In a moment we're engaged in a full-fledged water fight, laughing and shouting and splashing. Finally, her mother leans out the kitchen window and yells at us to quiet down.

Later Paulette offers to take me on a tour of the neighborhood. She has a lilting, musical voice; though my French is feeble, I have no trouble understanding her. While the others go hiking in the fields, we drive into the village in her old Simca. The houses of Parennes are crooked and lean against each other like old men. White curtains flutter in the open windows above boxes of brightly colored flowers. The streets are filled with people promenading in their Sunday best.

We drive past a large Gothic church, its tall bell tower adorned with fierce gargoyles. Behind the church is an old cemetery filled with ancient headstones. Paulette's family has lived here, attended this church, and been buried in this cemetery for hundreds of years, she says. They cannot imagine what it would be like to have to live under German rule. I hope they never have to find out.

As we drive along, I notice Paulette's skirt slowly creeping higher and higher up her legs. I can't help myself: I keep looking down at those beautiful legs of hers. Her skin is so white and so smooth. Her skirt is now above her knees. Would it be rude to just gently touch one of those knees with my hand? Or should I very slowly move over a little bit so that my knee might lean against hers as we come around a turn or hit a bump in the road? I'm so fascinated by those knees of hers that I almost forget to listen to what she is telling me about her family. What's the matter with me? We're supposed to be fighting a war, and all I can think about is girls.

On the way back to her house, we see Max and the others chasing a rabbit across a field. Without warning, Paulette guns the engine and turns the Simca off the road to join the hunt. We bounce across the field after the rabbit, the boys running alongside us, whooping and hollering, urging us to go faster. Finally, at the edge of the field, we stop. The boys fall to the ground, exhausted and laughing.

I get out of the car and jump on Max. "I've got a rabbit," I shout, "a nice big fat one, just right for dinner."

Max grins up at me. "And where have you and the Simca been all afternoon?" he asks. "Learning to park?"

Paulette blushes and says she'd better bring the car back before her father starts wondering where she is.

After she drives off, the teasing starts in earnest. "So, you want her all to yourself," Max leers. "While we're working hard chasing your supper, you're off chasing Paulette."

I try to make a joke of it, but I can't. Max is right. I really do like her.

To bed soon after dark. After a day of relaxation we must get an early start in the morning.

I lay awake on the living-room couch, staring at the ceiling, wondering if we'll ever get to Toulouse. And if we do, what will we find there?

I'm worried about my family. There's been virtually no news from home. They say the Belgian army has been putting up a good fight, but who knows what's really happening? Suddenly, I find myself feeling very lonely.

There are footsteps in the hall. It's Paulette. She stands in the entryway, peering in at me. "Are you awake?" she whispers.

I nod. She moves silently across the room and kneels by the couch. "I'm so afraid for you and your friends," she says. "Why can't people be left alone to live in peace?"

I tell her all we can do is try to end the war as quickly as possible.

She takes my hand. "Will you come back and see us?" she asks.

"Of course I will. We'll take the Simca and chase rabbits again." I pull her close and we kiss. She clings to me tightly for a long time.

I feel very warm inside. I can't believe that I actually kissed her. Or did she kiss me? Is this what people call love at first sight?

Finally, I push her away. "You'd better go to bed," I whisper, "or your parents won't let me come back here to visit you."

She rises and leaves the room. Somehow, I know I'll never see this place again.

May 27, 1940. Up early. After three cups of hot chocolate and a double helping of cottage cheese, we're on our way once more. Before long the grumbling starts up again. Lou is worried about what might be waiting for us down the road. He thinks we should find a place to stay and wait until we can get a train.

Paul agrees. "At the rate we're going," he says, "the war'll be over by the time we get to Toulouse."

By late afternoon we've ridden nearly one hundred kilometers. In the town of Sable we're told that we might be able to catch a train in Angers, about fifty kilometers south of here. We pedal on. Just before dark we reach Champagne. Marcel finds the mayor, who lets us sleep in the schoolhouse.

May 28, 1940. On the road early, with nothing to eat. At 8:00 A.M. we stop at a café in Maison St. Lucas and offer to earn our breakfast. The owner—a big, swarthy man in a leather apron, his shirt-sleeves rolled up on beefy arms—puts us to work sweeping the sidewalk and setting up tables out front.

The main topic of conversation among the customers is the war. The men don't have much to say, but the women (most of whose husbands seem to be off fighting on the Maginot Line) are quite vocal about how the German breakthrough is all the fault of Belgium. If Belgium hadn't refused to join up with Britain and France in September of 1939, they seem to believe, Europe might still be at peace.

Around 8:30 the owner shouts to us to come inside. The Belgian prime minister is speaking on the radio.

A dozen people are crowded around the radio at one end of the bar. An announcer is speaking in French. Marcel begins to translate: "King Leopold III has surrendered. The Belgian army has been ordered to lay down its weapons."

We look at each other in disbelief. How can this be true? Surely, the king would flee to England and form a government-in-exile rather than turn Belgium over to the Germans.

The other people in the café—mainly the women—begin to shout at us angrily. "We'd better get out of here," Max says. "Belgium was all that stood between them and the Germans."

I don't want to go anywhere. Why should we let a bunch of absurd Frenchwomen frighten us? "You're being absolutely ridiculous!" I shout at them. "Your own troops haven't exactly covered themselves with glory!"

Outside, people are beginning to gather in small groups, talking in excited voices. We start toward our bicycles but are quickly surrounded by a crowd of angry women. "Traitors!" they shout. "Cowards! What are you doing hiding in France? You should be at home fighting the Germans!"

One of the women picks up a large stone and shakes it in Lou's face. "This is what we should give you!" she shouts. "We'll show you how to fight like men!"

The café owner pushes his way through the crowd. "These are only young boys," he tells the angry women. "Leave them alone. Save your energy for the Germans."

We jump on our bikes and pedal off as fast as we can. "Maybe we *should* go back home," Lou says. "The Germans couldn't treat us any worse than the French."

He's talking nonsense. Our only hope is to get to Toulouse as quickly as we can.

We ride into Angers a few hours later and head straight for the police station. When we tell the sergeant behind the desk who we are and where we're going, he shakes his head. "You'd better be careful," he warns us. "People around here are very angry about what happened in Belgium."

He promises to find us a train as soon as possible. In the meantime, we are to stay in the station for our own protection.

We're put in a large, locked room with folding cots. Lou and Josef immediately start complaining. Around 9:00 P.M. a police inspector comes in. He looks shaken and angry. The Germans, he says, have cut across France to the coast. Boulogne has fallen, and Calais is under attack. The French and British armies are trapped at Dunkerque.

The inspector takes off his cap and sighs. He has arranged for us to join a troop train that should get us to Toulouse by the morning. "I was in the last war," he says. "It was terrible." He stares at us for a moment, then leaves.

Just after midnight we're taken to the station by a tight-lipped police-man. A train is waiting at the platform, its windows blacked out against the Luftwaffe. The policeman raps on the door to the baggage car. "Open up in there!" he shouts. "I've got some baggage for Tou-louse."

The door is opened by an old man, who helps us load our luggage and bicycles into the car. We're to ride in the baggage car as well. "For your own good," the old man explains. "Belgians aren't too popular in France right now."

We stretch out on some mailbags. A few minutes later the train lurches into motion.

Chapter Two

Soldier in Training

May 29, 1940. We arrive in Toulouse just before noon, tired, thirsty, and hungry. At the city hall in the Place du Capitole, we're told to report to an armory on the outskirts of town—the new temporary headquarters of the Belgian army.

Recruits are drilling on a dusty parade ground in front of the armory. While we wait to be processed, we sprawl on the porch of the old stone building, watching them. I hate to say it, but they're not very impressive.

After about twenty minutes, I'm called inside to be interviewed by a Belgian officer. He says my friends and I have done well to have gotten as far as we have. Then he looks at my papers and asks about my studies at the university. When I finish telling him about my background, he nods and says we're to go to a camp that's been set up on the grounds of a chateau in Lussan, about thirty-five kilometers west of here.

There are several such camps (formally known as Belgian Army Recruiting Centres) in the area, he tells me. With officers in terribly short supply, he adds, the army is looking for young men who have university degrees or are working on them to help run these camps as platoon chiefs. "There are already about 150 young men at Lussan," he says. "It's a bit of a shambles—no officers or any kind of discipline.

I'd like you to take charge and get things organized. Think you're
up to it?"

I straighten up proudly and accept his offer on the spot. Of course
I'm up to it. After all, this won't be the first time I've been placed
in a position of leadership. Almost invariably, whenever I joined a
club or organization, it wouldn't be long before I became secretary
or vice-president or even president of the group. I enjoy running
things.

The boys and I reach Lussan early in the afternoon. The chateau
sits in a fertile valley dotted with large farms. It's a handsome building,
with a broad terrace running along the front and impressive stone
pillars flanking the entrance.

A flock of geese is blocking the main gate. We ride on through,
and the birds scatter, sending up a loud cackle to announce our
arrival.

An elderly woman wearing a black dress and a shawl is standing
out front, watching us. I hand her the papers that authorize me to
take over the chateau. She glances at them and shrugs. I take the
papers back and give them to Marcel. "By order of the French and
Belgian governments," he reads aloud in his nearly perfect French,
"the Chateau de Lussan will serve as a recruiting center for the
Belgian army."

The old woman shakes her head in a mixture of amusement and
disdain. "It's about time," she says. "Your charges are in the barn.
Maybe you can make them behave."

The barn is on a hill behind the chateau. We walk up and find a
raggedy group of young men sitting around an open fire in the barn-
yard, cooking a pig on a spit. I show my papers to a tall, rangy
fellow who is picking at the carcass with a knife. He doesn't seem
to be impressed by my authority. "If you're going to be our chief,"
he says, "the first thing you can do is find us some food."

His mates start to laugh. "That's right, chief," one of them shouts.
"Find us some food."

I send Max down to the chateau to get a pencil and some paper
so we can draw up a list of everyone in the camp. The first priority
is to bring some order to this chaos.

It takes us an hour or so to round up everyone. As the officer in Toulouse said, the camp is a shambles. The men have been left completely to their own devices, living off the land, begging for bread and vegetables during the day, stealing pigs and chickens at night.

When the group is all assembled, I remind them what we're doing here. We are guests in France, and we must act like guests. That means no more stealing from the local farmers. From now on, I tell them, we'll either pay or work for all the food we eat.

"Easy for you to say," shouts the tall one with the knife, "but we can't eat words. We need food."

"You'll get food," I shout back, "but you'll get it honestly."

I send Marcel off on his bicycle to make the rounds of the local farmers to see if any of them need extra laborers. It turns out they all do.

After dinner, I divide the group into five platoons. I appoint Paul— the tall one with the knife—leader of the first platoon, which will be responsible for gathering and preparing all our food. The other four platoons will report to Marcel in the morning and will be assigned to work on the farms.

May 30, 1940. Up early to send the platoons off to work. A dozen stragglers refuse to go. I tell them they can stay in the barn as long as they like, but anyone who doesn't work won't eat.

I assign Paul's platoon to clean up the camp. They take great pleasure in throwing the lazy ones out of the barn. Two of the laggards change their mind and join Paul's platoon. The rest wander off on their own.

I spend the day waiting for orders from headquarters in Toulouse. I'm hoping they'll also send us some money so we can buy provisions.

At dusk, the four work platoons return from the fields. They bring with them enough vegetables and bread to take care of tonight's dinner, as well as tomorrow's breakfast.

Unfortunately, the farmers won't give us any meat or poultry. According to Marcel, they claim our men have already stolen more pigs, chickens, and geese than they can afford to give up. Marcel adds that there was a lot of grumbling on the way back. Few of our men are used to field work. City boys.

May 31, 1940. Twenty-three men refuse to get up for work this morning. What's worse, the ones who didn't work yesterday look suspiciously well fed. I send an urgent request to Toulouse for money and orders.

At midmorning Paul warns me that trouble is brewing. The laggards, he reports, were out stealing food last night. Now they're evidently bragging that they've found a place to steal some wine. "They won't leave the barn," he says, "and I'm not sure I can get my men to throw them out."

I tell him to get a strong stick and follow me. If his men are afraid to throw those pigs out, we'll do it ourselves. One thing I've learned is that lazy people are usually cowards. All you have to do is stand up to them, and they break.

We arrive at the barn to find Paul's platoon crowded around the entrance. I walk inside—and am immediately pelted with sticks and pebbles. "We didn't come here to become farm workers," yells one of the laggards. He steps out of the crowd and glowers at me. He is a couple of years older than me, with a crooked nose (from the looks of it, the result of a poorly healed break). "If these farmers want us to protect them from the Germans," he says, "they should be willing to feed us."

I hold up my stick. "I want all of you outside," I shout. "Now!"

No one moves. Broken Nose grins at me. "How 'bout if I throw *you* out of here?" he says.

He raises his fists and rushes toward me. I evade him easily, driving the end of my stick into his midsection. He doubles over, gasping for breath. I dance around him and swat him in the back of the knees. He crumples to the ground.

I stand over him. "Can you leave on your own," I ask, "or would you like some help?" He glances up at me and scurries out the door, followed by his mates. Paul's platoon cheers.

In the afternoon Marcel appears with more bad news. The farmers lost more chickens last night and are starting to think the only reason we've offered to work for them is so we can scout out their farms to steal from them at night. Two say they won't take any more of our workers in the future.

To make matters worse, Broken Nose and two dozen others disappear just before dinner. Obviously, they've gone off to steal food.

I call the remaining men together after dinner. I thank them for working so hard, then bring up the farmers' complaints. "We cannot allow the stealing to continue," I tell them. "Those who refuse to work will have to be locked up at night."

Later, Paul takes me aside and suggests that I sleep in the chateau. Word is that Broken Nose and his mates are planning to get me after everyone is asleep. "There's a lot of resentment," he says. "It's not safe for you in the barn."

I don't want to be separated from the men, but what can I do? I move into the chateau.

June 1, 1940. More than thirty men refuse to go to work this morning. They've been drinking, and when Paul tries to get them to leave the barn, they drive him off with rocks. I tell him to arm his platoon with sticks and lock the laggards in.

At noon Marcel brings fifty men back from the fields. The farmers don't want them, he reports. As I feared, there was more stealing last night. Among other things, a wine cellar was looted.

As a result, we have barely enough food for dinner. I'm still waiting for word from Toulouse. What can be going on at headquarters? The officer who gave me my assignment clearly said that a regular army officer would be stopping by to check on us the day following my arrival, and that we would be provided with all sorts of food.

The officer also showed a map on which were marked the dozen or so other recruiting centers in the area. Some of the centers had numbers, such as the 533d at L'Isle Arne and the 541st in Marsan. Lussan was not one of them.

I can't figure out what is happening. Not only are we not getting any food or supplies, headquarters isn't even answering my messages. The old woman at the chateau told me that the last time she had seen any Belgian officers at Lussan was a couple of days before I arrived.

I'm tempted to get on my bicycle and ride to Toulouse myself. But getting there and back will take two full days, and I don't think it's a good idea for me to be gone for so long. I go to bed (once again, in the chateau) deeply discouraged.

Max wakes me up in the middle of the night. The laggards have broken out of the barn and taken fifty more men with them. They've gone off to steal more food and wine—after which they evidently intend to come back and take care of me.

I tell Max to get Paul and as many of the others as he can and bring them up to the chateau. He returns with just thirty-five men. Paul is not among them—he wants to wait and see what happens before taking sides.

June 2, 1940. At dawn I send Max to Toulouse to get help. Broken Nose and his friends are nowhere in sight.

After breakfast, I lead my men up the hill to see what's going on in the barn. Halfway up, we are driven back by a hail of stones. We retreat to the chateau and lock the doors.

For the next two hours all is quiet. Then a rock crashes through a window in the kitchen. Broken Nose and his men—nearly a hundred of them—are gathered in the courtyard, armed with sticks and clubs. "Hey, Vandermeerssche," he shouts, "why don't you come out and show us how tough you are?"

"Are you all crazy?" I yell back. "If you keep this up, we'll have the whole countryside after us. We're here to fight the Germans, not each other."

Broken Nose doesn't reply.

"Throw down your sticks," I continue, "and I'll come out, and we can talk it over."

"Sure," Broken Nose shouts, "whatever you say."

I start for the door. Marcel stops me. "You won't last two minutes out there," he says. "He wants revenge, and they want to watch."

Marcel means well, but I have no choice. If I go out now, it'll be just me against Broken Nose. If I don't, they'll all break in, and we'll have a whole mob to deal with.

I take a deep breath and walk outside. Broken Nose is grinning and rubbing his large hands together.

I stare at him evenly. He stares back, then charges, arms reaching for me. I duck under him and toss a handful of dirt in his face. Blinded, he stumbles and falls on his face. Everyone bursts out laughing.

Slowly, he gets to his feet, pawing the ground like a maddened bull. He's not about to give up—not with everyone watching. I'm beginning to think this may not end until one of us is badly hurt, maybe even dead.

Suddenly, we hear the blare of an automobile horn. A large, black staff car is bouncing up the road toward the chateau. Max is clinging to the running board, grinning broadly.

The car pulls into the courtyard, and a Belgian officer in a khaki field uniform jumps out. He pushes his way through the crowd of rebels, his hand resting lightly on the butt of a pistol strapped to his hip. "This garrison is being disbanded," the officer shouts. "All companies line up immediately!"

Grumbling and shoving, the men form ragged, uneven lines. The officer surveys them sourly, then turns to me and in a low voice explains that I'm to take about half the group to the camp that has been established at the chateau at L'Isle Arne. The rest are to go to Marsan. "Pick whom you please," he says. "You've earned the privilege."

The officer goes into the chateau. I walk over to Max, who is standing by the car, and shake his hand. "Your timing couldn't have been better," I tell him.

He grins at me. In all the confusion, headquarters had simply forgotten about us. "They were furious when I told them what was going on here," he says.

I select sixty men to make the twenty-kilometer trek to L'Isle Arne, where we're to join the 533d Infantry Company. We march out of Lussan at noon, under a bright sun, following the narrow, dusty road up into the hills above the chateau.

It's late in the afternoon, and we're tired and thirsty by the time we arrive at our destination. L'Isle Arne is a much grander chateau than Lussan, with tall, shuttered windows and its own chapel. As we march through the main gate into the courtyard, I notice a dozen small children and teenage girls watching us.

Inside, I'm introduced to the company commandant, a one-legged veteran of the last war named Albert Castiaux. Castiaux's bearing is all military—right down to the aristocratic handlebar mustache—but his voice is friendly. He questions me about the problems at Lussan, then asks about my studies at the university, raising an eyebrow when I tell him of my interest in mathematics and how I've been tutoring older students since I was eleven.

I'm to be in charge of the 5th Platoon, he says. I hope there won't be any discipline problems here.

June 3, 1940. Awakened early by a trumpet sounding reveille. First order of business is calisthenics in the courtyard. After breakfast, we're put to work digging a latrine. For the first time I truly feel like a soldier.

Everything is so well organized. Real military discipline. I wonder how Broken Nose and the rest of the guys I sent to Marsan are handling it.

At noon we're called back to the courtyard. As the entire camp watches, one of the cooks carries a steaming bowl of fresh soup out of the Cuisine d'Armée—a large, mobile kitchen parked next to the chateau—and presents it to Commandant Castiaux. With great ceremony, Castiaux raises a spoonful to his lips, tasting it carefully, as if it were a rare vintage wine. Finally, he nods his approval, and we're ordered to line up for lunch.

According to the other platoon chiefs, Castiaux does this before every meal. He obviously takes a great interest in how his men are fed.

June 5, 1940. The routine here is simple and exhausting. Up early for calisthenics, then breakfast, then some work assignment: cleaning up the grounds, hauling water, gathering wood for the cooking fires. After lunch we drill in the courtyard, learning the rudiments of soldiering. Then more chores, followed by supper and finally sleep.

There are some 350 men here at L'Isle Arne. In addition, both Commandant Castiaux and his number two, M. Desobry, have their families with them (in all fifteen children, ranging in age from three to seventeen). We see the families occasionally, mainly at mealtimes, but fraternization is discouraged.

June 6, 1940. This morning after breakfast I'm called into Commandant Castiaux's office. He says he's been watching me with the men, and he likes my combination of discipline and fairness. As a result, he's decided to give me some additional assignments. "Starting tomorrow," he says, "you'll be in charge of the kitchen."

I protest that I know nothing about cooking.

"That's what the cooks are for," he replies. "Your job will be to manage them and to gather the food."

He has another new assignment for me as well. When I ask what it is, he gets up and tells me to follow him. We walk down a corridor to a large, musty room with a high ceiling and tall, narrow windows covered with heavy drapes.

"We need someone to teach the children," he says. "This will be your classroom."

I stare at him. I left home to become a soldier, to fight for my country—not to work in a kitchen and tutor children.

Castiaux ignores my unhappy look. "The children will be brought down shortly," he says, then turns and leaves.

I walk to the window and fling open the drapes. Out in the courtyard men are marching. What am I doing in here?

There are footsteps behind me. I turn to find a tall, slender blonde girl of about seventeen or so standing in the doorway. "Monsieur Vandermeerssche?" she asks with a grin. "Your platoon is reporting for duty."

She ushers in a group of seven teenagers, calling out their names as they enter the room: "Jeannine, Violette, Charles, Rene . . ." Finally, she introduces herself. She is Raymonde Desobry, eldest daughter of Castiaux's number two. She smiles at me warmly. I smile back. Perhaps this tutoring won't be so bad after all.

June 13, 1940. How quickly one falls into a routine. Every morning I rise before dawn to check on things in the mobile kitchen. Then off on my bicycle to buy fresh fruit and vegetables in one of the nearby villages. According to Commandant Castiaux, good food is the key to good morale. (It helps that the cooks are all Flemish like me; we speak each other's language in more ways than one.)

Later in the day I give the teenagers their lessons. While the older ones work, the younger children play outside. Sometimes I entertain them with magic tricks I learned from my uncle. Raymonde helps out, acting as a kind of mother to the little ones. Every once in a while I catch her staring at me. I wink, and she grins back. There's something happening between us, no question about it.

June 20, 1940. The war news is discouraging. Paris fell last week, and there are rumors that Hitler himself showed up in the Arc de Triomphe to review his troops. They also say Marshal Pétain has formed a new French government in Vichy.

June 21, 1940. I've taken to visiting the kitchen in the chateau, where Raymonde helps her mother and the other women prepare meals for their families. I sit next to her, and we talk while she peels potatoes and cleans vegetables.

June 22, 1940. Pétain has signed an armistice with Hitler. No one knows what it will mean for us.

June 24, 1940. I drop in on Raymonde in the chateau kitchen. We talk for a bit while she peels some carrots. Suddenly, she grabs my hand and asks me if I think we'll ever get back to Belgium.

"Of course," I say.

"And what will you do then?"

I think I know what she's asking. "Oh," I reply casually, "I suppose I'll go back to the university."

Raymonde frowns and looks down at the table.

"And I'll come visit you in Biez," I quickly add.

She grins and blushes. Women.

July 8, 1940. I'm worried about my family. My mother has written to me, but the mail from Belgium is censored, and I can't be sure everything is as fine as she says. The news on the official French radio is useless. They just spout Nazi propaganda. I'm beginning to wonder if I should leave L'Isle Arne and go home to see for myself how things are. If it's true—as some are saying—that the German occupation isn't all that bad, perhaps I could go back to school and finish my studies.

No, that's nonsense. The only way I'll go back to Belgium is as a liberator. But what good am I doing here? Perhaps I should try to get across the border to Spain. From there I could make my way to England. With my technical background, I'm certain I could qualify for pilot training in the Royal Air Force.

July 13, 1940. Fresh meat is getting harder to find, and prices are soaring. To make matters worse, headquarters is sending us less money than ever. Raymonde says her father told her that Commandant Castiaux has been paying for our provisions out of his own pocket.

July 15, 1940. It's been raining for the last few days. As a result, we've all been forced to stay inside, and morale is poor. Last night a fight broke out in the 1st Platoon. The men got into the food stores and threw potatoes at each other.

July 16, 1940. After breakfast, Commandant Castiaux assembles everyone in the courtyard to find out who started the fight Sunday night. He asks each member of the 1st Platoon what happened. No one will say anything.

Enraged, Castiaux orders the entire platoon to be put on half rations. I can't understand him sometimes. Does he really think that denying the men food will help matters?

July 18, 1940. We've run out of firewood. I distribute axes to my men and take them down the road to ask the neighboring landowners if we can remove fallen trees from their property.

The men grumble as they work. Morale is dangerously low. If something's not done, who knows what might happen?

In the afternoon I go to see Commandant Castiaux to warn him about the mood of the men. It turns out he's aware of the problem. In fact, he expects things to get worse. The Germans, he says gloomily, are pressuring the Vichy government to close down the camp and send us home. All we can do, he sighs, is take each day as it comes.

Then he brightens and asks me if I know what day this coming Sunday is. I think for a minute. It's July 21—Independence Day! Of course. We can organize a celebration. Perhaps that will help morale.

July 19, 1940. We begin preparations for the Independence Day fête. The mess hall is decorated with garlands of flowers and boughs

of evergreen. On one wall we hang a large white banner that reads:
"Vive Notre Commandant!"

Madame L'Espinasse, the caretaker of the chateau, searches
through the vast attic and finds enough white tablecloths to cover
every table in the mess hall. Even the children are put to work—
copying the menu of the day in pen and ink on heavy white paper.
There will be one for every place, with each man's name individually
inscribed.

July 21, 1940. Independence Day. Commandant Castiaux addresses
the men at breakfast. "This day carries special meaning for us," he
says, "because it brings us closer together in a strange land. We
are all patriots in exile, and our hearts yearn for our homeland."

After breakfast, we gather in the courtyard to watch as delegations
of men from each platoon lay wreaths on the monument to the soldiers
who died in the 1914–18 war. Then, as the bugler plays taps, we
run up the Belgian flag and the French tricolor.

Later we gather in the valley below the chateau. A cattle wagon
is pulled in to serve as a stage, and a recruit with a fine tenor voice
sings patriotic songs. It's very moving. By the time the singer is
finished, many of the men are crying.

I feel like crying myself. My mother has a wonderful voice, and
good singing always reminds me of her. She once told Simone and
me that when she was a young girl, her dream had been to become
an opera singer. Unfortunately, her father, who was very strict, for-
bade it—on the grounds that "those sort of people are not serious."
As far as he was concerned, she would be much better off becoming
a teacher like him and her older sisters. Mother was an obedient
girl, and she dutifully followed her father's instructions. Nonetheless,
I think she knows just about every classical opera word for word in
its original language. (I could never understand why parents don't
let their children choose their own careers. After all, they're the
children's own futures.)

I share my mother's love of classical music, piano music in particular.
I've always wished I could play the piano myself. Indeed, after saving
money for months, I finally took my first piano lesson at the beginning
of May. Then, of course, the Germans invaded, and who knows if
I'll ever get to take another one.

We return to the mess hall at 2:00 P.M. for dinner. The men are delighted by the individual menus. Songs and laughter fill the huge room. After the last course, Lambory, the adjutant, proposes a toast to Commandant Castiaux. The men roar their approval.

At dusk we return to the valley, where a giant bonfire has been lit. The children beg me to perform some of my magic tricks. Reluctantly, I agree. Soon the entire camp is watching. I manage to get through my routine without any mishaps and am rewarded with a huge round of applause.

Embarrassed, I slip back into the crowd and sit down next to Raymonde. Once again, a singer takes the stage. His voice echoes through the valley, accompanied by the crackling and snapping of the fire.

As the sun goes down, I put my arm around Raymonde. She moves close, shivering slightly in the cool night breeze. I too am trembling.

I feel so incredibly close to her. I don't think I've ever felt this way about anyone before.

July 22, 1940. First thing after breakfast a truck filled with French soldiers pulls into the courtyard. The soldiers go into the chateau, emerging a few minutes later with Commandant Castiaux. "They are here to take the Cuisine d'Armée," he tells me. "They say they need it back."

The mobile kitchen is hitched to the truck and driven off. The cooks are furious. Now they'll have to do all their cooking on the fireplace in the chateau kitchen.

July 26, 1940. There are conflicting reports on how the war is going. Some letters from home make it sound as if everything's perfectly normal. Others talk about food shortages and "ersatz" coffee.

July 28, 1940. Commandant Castiaux calls me into his office and tells me to shut the door. He's received word that the Germans have formally asked the French to send all refugees home. "I don't expect the Vichy government to do much to protect us," he says. "We must start planning for our departure."

July 30, 1940. Rumors are circulating that a train is waiting in Aubiet to take us all home. Should I be excited? Grateful? Relieved? I feel none of these things. Only a profound depression.

July 31, 1940. We spend the day cleaning up the chateau and packing our belongings. After supper Commandant Castiaux addresses the men. "The French Vichy government and the Belgian government of the occupation have jointly ordered us to return to our homes," he says. "In the morning you will march to Aubiet, where you will board the train for Belgium. You should all be home within three days." He adds that the occupation seems to be going smoothly, and that the German army has been treating our women and children with respect.

Most of the men are overjoyed. They can't believe they'll be back with their families, sleeping in their own beds, in just a few days. I, too, miss my parents and sister. But somehow this doesn't seem right.

I tag along after Castiaux as he walks back to the chateau. "I'm not sure I want to go back home," I tell him. "I've been thinking about escaping across the mountains into Spain and joining the Allied armies in England."

Castiaux stares off into space for a moment. "I know how you must feel," he says finally. "But you've been ordered to return to Belgium, and a soldier must obey his orders. It's your duty to return."

I start to protest, but he interrupts me. "If we don't obey," he says, "who knows what they might do to our families?"

August 1, 1940. I'm up most of the night with the cooks, preparing coffee and food for our early-morning departure. After breakfast, the entire company lines up in the courtyard so Commandant Castiaux can address us for the last time. "You have all been loyal Belgians," he says, "and I thank you for that. I expect you will all conduct yourselves as well on the trip home and see that everyone makes it safely."

His voice falters at the end. For a moment we all stand there silently. Then a loud cheer goes up. As we march out of L'Isle Arne, many of the men are singing, happy to be on their way home at last.

We reach Aubiet late in the afternoon. Our train consists of a string of boxcars. The cooks and I are put in a car literally filled with hundreds of small, round loaves of bread—the company's food for the journey. There's no place to sit but on the bread, and before long a few of the cooks are sprawled asleep on the loaves, exhausted by the long march and lulled by the rocking of the train.

As we travel north, closer and closer to German-occupied territory, I find myself growing more and more worried. Perhaps this is a German trick. Perhaps we're not going home at all. There've been rumors about German slave-labor camps that use civilians from the occupied countries. They take healthy young people and then slowly work them to death.

What if this train's destination isn't really Belgium, but some labor camp in Germany?

Shortly before midnight the train slows, then comes to a halt. I can hear soldiers outside shouting in German. A moment later the doors slide open, and three German officers wearing black swastika armbands peer in at us. "Everyone out for inspection!" one of them barks.

I was right. We've been tricked. I'll never see my family again.

Shivering in the cool night air, we line up next to the tracks. I've never seen German soldiers before. In their tall-peaked caps, smart gray uniforms, and polished black boots, they seem larger than life. The officer reads off our names from a list. Then, in a businesslike tone, he asks us about our supply of food. When someone complains that we have nothing to drink, he instructs one of his men to fill our canteens.

Finally, we're told to reboard the train. "You're going back to Belgium to be part of a new order," the officer says. "Tomorrow you'll be with your families. Have a good trip."

August 2, 1940. Dawn. We're rattling through the suburbs of Paris. Through the partially open door, I can see houses and villages rushing past.

As I watch, the landscape changes, growing flatter, more rural, blanketed with a patchwork of small farms. The fields are covered with golden summer wheat and sprinkled with blue cornflowers and red poppies.

Late afternoon. The train slows. We're passing a customs station. This must be the border! A cheer goes up. We're in Belgium! Home at last!

Everyone in the car crowds around the door, shouting and laughing, reading aloud from familiar billboards that none of us have seen in months. Then silence, as we pass a long row of bombed-out buildings, their collapsed walls revealing charred interiors littered with rubble and smashed furniture.

The train stops in a village, next to a badly damaged bridge. In the distance we hear men singing a capella in a foreign tongue. The voices grow louder, accompanied by the staccato pounding of hobnail boots on a cobblestone street. Finally, we see a company of German soldiers marching four abreast up a road near the tracks. "Wir fahren gegen England," they sing. "We're on our way to England."

"Look at them!" shouts someone in the car. "You never saw French soldiers marching like that."

The remark shocks me. So what if they can march and sing well? They are the enemy, the ones who took our freedom away.

The train starts up again. I can't take my eyes off the Germans. The precision of these gray-uniformed soldiers, the power in their young voices—it's terrifying.

We cross Belgium at a snail's pace. Every five minutes, it seems, we're shunted onto a siding to allow a German troop train to pass. The country looks pretty much the same as it did when I left— except for the occasional bombed-out village and the many German soldiers I see guarding the stations and the main highway crossings.

We pull into Brussels's South Station just after dusk. The waiting room is crowded with relatives. They spill onto the platform, excitedly pushing their way past the Wehrmacht guards. This annoys the Germans, and they refuse to let us off the train until the platform is cleared.

Though I'm not expecting anyone to meet me here, I find myself overwhelmed by a wave of loneliness and homesickness. After a few last good-byes, I make my way to the train for Ghent and sleep most of the way there.

I'm filled with happiness as I walk home from Sint Pieter Station. War or no war, Ghent doesn't seem to have changed a bit. Then I turn the corner of Ieperenstraat and find a German soldier pointing a rifle at my chest.

"Papieren!" he demands.

I hand him my travel documents. He examines them, then waves me on.

I hurry down the street, frightened and angry.

When I reach my front door, I stick my hand through the letter slot and bang the bronze hinge back and forth. It's the secret signal I've used since I was a small boy to let my mother know I'm home.

A moment later she flings the door open, staring at me as if I'm a ghost. "It's him!" she shouts. "Gaston is home!" She hugs me tightly, laughing and crying at the same time, then leads me into the kitchen, where Pa and Simone are waiting.

We talk late into the night. Pa says he's surprised to see me. He thought I'd be in England by now.

That makes me feel good. It means he had faith in me, that he assumed I wouldn't turn into a black- or brown-shirted collaborator like so many of my generation. Even in our own family, it seems, several of my cousins didn't waste any time enrolling in one of the Nazi youth organizations.

Chapter Three

Resistance

August 6, 1940. The night I came home, Pa warned me I wouldn't believe what's been happening here. He was right. There are Wehrmacht soldiers everywhere, strutting through our streets as if they owned them, crowding all the stores and buying merchandise as if there were no tomorrow. You can see them in the post offices sending hundreds and hundreds of parcels back home to the "fatherland." While the Germans can buy anything they want, we need special stamps to purchase even the barest of necessities.

Even worse is the sight of young Belgians marching through the city, wearing black or brown shirts with Nazi swastikas on their arms and singing German songs. It makes me sick.

August 18, 1940. Today is my nineteenth birthday—not a particularly happy occasion. I've decided to go back to the university in the fall. I should be able to get a position as an assistant to one of the instructors. What else can I do, really?

August 24, 1940. The Nazis have stepped up their propaganda, urging the Flemish people to join with them in a spirit of new racial pride and unity. Their latest project is a campaign calling for the elimination of French as a language of commerce and public life. Needless to say, they want to replace it with German.

Pa says the Germans tried this sort of thing during the last war—
attacking our national unity by playing on the feeling that we Flemish
are basically German, while the Walloons are at bottom French.

September 3, 1940. According to the BBC, the British Royal Air
Force is holding its own against the Luftwaffe. Still, the German
blitz is taking a terrible toll on London.

Things here are very gloomy. The Germans arrest people on the
flimsiest of pretexts and send them off to work camps. Even listening
to the BBC has become dangerous. The Germans are jamming it
with a distinctive high-pitched signal that makes listening extremely
difficult and detection frighteningly easy.

The Jews, who must now wear large yellow stars on their coats
or face deportation, are being rounded up like cattle. The Nazis
say they're turning each other in so they can steal each other's property. This can't be true.

I don't know any Jews myself. Ghent isn't like Antwerp, where
the diamond-cutting industry is located. There are very few Jews
here. I guess I've never paid much attention to them one way or
the other. What I can't understand is why the Germans are singling
them out so viciously—and why the Jews are letting them get away
with it. If I were Jewish, I wouldn't wear a yellow star. I'd go into
hiding first or escape to Free France or Spain or England.

September 18, 1940. The Germans have thrown up roadblocks on
all the main roads to stop black marketeers from bringing real food
into the city. I think the idea is to make us too weak to resist.

Whatever the intention, meat and fresh vegetables have all but
disappeared. The bread we get is a dark, gooey mess that looks
and tastes like it's made from brown paint and sawdust. The stuff
sticks to the knife like putty. In fact, you need two knives to slice
it—one to do the actual cutting, the other to scrape the slice off
the first knife.

How I regret my decision to come home.

September 25, 1940. The university has rejected my application to
become a teaching assistant. Just like that. With no explanation.

September 26, 1940. I can't believe it. They've appointed Arnold as
a teaching assistant. He's done nothing to deserve the post except

learn how to be a good little Nazi. They seem to be rewarding everyone who stayed behind when we left for France.

Marcel warns me to watch what I say. The Germans are arresting anyone even suspected of resisting. Our leftist friend Frans was picked up right after the invasion. According to Marcel, he's been sent to a salt mine in Germany.

October 3, 1940. The Nazis are really cracking down. Today they ordered all Belgian men between the ages of eighteen and fifty— and all unmarried women between twenty-one and thirty-five—to register for some kind of war service. There are Hitler Youth in all my classes.

Why didn't I trust my instincts and try to get to England instead of coming back here?

October 5, 1940. I've resumed my math tutoring. I figure I can handle about ten private students a month. I'd rather not do it, but with all the scholarships going to collaborators, I really don't have any choice.

October 12, 1940. Pa must sense my growing desire to do something to resist the Nazis. After supper he takes me aside and warns me against getting involved in any activities directed against the occupation troops. "You don't know the Germans, but I do," he says. "They're ruthless and vicious. They tolerate no one who disobeys. For those who work against them, there is only one punishment—death."

I say nothing. "If you won't think of yourself," Pa continues, looking sad and tired, "think of your mother and sister. Remember, if the Germans can't find you, your family is next."

My father is a strange man. He's tough and stern—stubborn, really. When he thinks he's right, he won't budge. Take his refusal to pay bribes to get government contracts for his carpentry shop. Or his atheism—which, over the years, has cost him a lot of customers. Another man might bend, compromise, pretend to be a good Catholic for the sake of the business. But not Pa. He just gets more determined. How often I have heard him shout, "It's dishonest and unjust, and I will not give in!"

Yet now he's telling me to do just that. We've never really talked about his experiences fighting the Germans in the last war. (We never really talk about anything at length.) Judging from the scared look on his face and the deep sadness in his eyes these days, it must have been terrible.

I do know that he spent four years in the trenches near the coast. He once told me a story about being sent on some sort of courier assignment and mistakenly crossing into enemy territory. When he realized where he was, he was scared to death. I remember how surprised I was when he told me that: I didn't know, nor did I believe, that my father could be afraid of anything.

There was another war story he told me—about nearly being burned alive. Pa suffered from bad teeth, and so he always carried tablets of potassium chlorate, which he used to relieve the pain. One day he was near the front lines, delivering a message to an officer. As he stood at attention in front of the officer, he felt a sharp pain in his side. With the officer standing over him, however, he didn't dare look, or even feel with his hand, to see what was wrong. Instead, he just stood there, trying to ignore the pain. Suddenly, to his astonishment, the officer pushed him into a bomb pit filled with mud and water. What had happened was that his potassium pills had accidentally rubbed against a matchbox and burst into flame.

These fragments are just about all he's been willing to tell me about "his" war. There must have been so much more to it than that. But what? I have so many questions. Here we are in a war again—once again with the Germans as our enemies. Surely there was something we should have learned from the last war. Why the Germans again? Are they so very different from us?

October 16, 1940. By bicycle to Uccle, a pleasant little town about fifteen kilometers southeast of Brussels, where Commandant Castiaux and his family live. The commandant is delighted to see me. At first we talk about our families and my studies at the university. Then, as if he can read my mind, he asks me what's wrong.

I explain how I've come to regret returning home.

"You did the right thing," he insists. "You have no idea how vindictive the Germans can be." Just yesterday, he tells me, someone attacked a Wehrmacht soldier in Brussels. In retaliation, the Germans arrested twenty-five hostages. Starting tomorrow, they're going to begin executing five of them each day until whoever was responsible for the attack gives himself up.

I can't believe this sort of thing can happen. "Isn't there anything anyone can do?" I ask Castiaux.

"Such as what?" he snaps. "Kill another German soldier—so they can slaughter twenty-five more hostages?"

I have no answer. "I want to go to England and join the Allied army," I say finally. "I want to fight them on even terms."

Castiaux's expression softens. "If you feel you must fight, then you must fight," he says. "But remember, you must also protect your family."

After saying good-bye to Commandant Castiaux, I decide to ride on to Biez, where Raymonde's family lives. Her younger brothers and sisters are playing in the front yard, and they start shouting my name as I ride up. Raymonde comes running from the house.

She looks wonderful. "Have you come to give us a lesson?" she asks with a grin. "Or did you think we missed your cooking?"

We go for a walk. Compared to Ghent or Brussels, there are hardly any Germans in Biez—though I do notice a growing military presence at a small airfield on the outskirts of the town.

As we stroll past the airfield, I tell her about my desire to get to England and join the RAF.

Raymonde seems surprised that I might want to leave school. I explain that the university is being taken over by Nazis. If you're a good little Hitler Youth, you get ahead. Otherwise, forget it.

"But what if you get caught?" she asks. "You'd be arrested and sent away."

She doesn't seem to understand. "Things won't be right in Belgium until we drive the Germans out," I tell her. "We've got to find ways to help the Allies. Like giving them information. Take this airfield, for example. You could watch it—keep track of which aircraft come and go."

Raymonde stops walking and stands there, staring at me. "Do you know what you're saying?" she asks in a small, shocked voice. "Don't you know what they do to spies?"

Now it's my turn to be surprised. What's happened to the self-assured young woman I felt so close to at L'Isle Arne? Raymonde

seems to have turned into a frightened little girl—someone I hardly
know. The war that threw us together now seems to be pulling us
apart.

October 20, 1940. For the past few days I've been keeping my ears
open, asking cautious questions, trying to find someone who can
get me in touch with the underground. I'm pretty sure my friend
Julien works with them, but I must be careful. I've heard that the
Germans use double agents to catch people like me.

October 22, 1940. At school this morning I ask Julien to meet me
after class in a park by the canal. He shows up right on time.
   "I know you're in the underground," I tell him. "I want to help."
   Julien regards me thoughtfully for a moment, then nods. He's
known me a long time and has been expecting this. "Tomorrow,"
he instructs me, "leave your books on the floor after class. I'll put
the latest issue of *La Libre Belgique* between them. Find a way to
make copies and circulate them among people you trust."
   That should be easy. There's an old mimeograph machine in our
attic, a leftover from my mother's days as a schoolteacher. And my
father has a typewriter I can use.
   I tell Julien he can count on me. He nods somberly. "This is the
last time we'll meet in public," he says.

October 23, 1940. At last I am doing something! In the morning,
as agreed, I leave my books on the floor of the lecture hall. When
I return to get them, there's a copy of *La Libre Belgique* hidden in
the pile.
   After my parents go to bed, I slip into my father's small office
just off the first-floor landing and start typing up stencils for the
mimeo. By midnight I have run off fifty copies of the paper.
   La Libre Belgique was started right after the German occupation
began. It appears irregularly, usually about every ten days or so,
reporting all the uncensored political, economic, and military news
it can get—much of it from the BBC in London. In addition to
including articles written by prominent politicians who are currently
"underground," the paper also warns patriots about suspected double
agents. It is printed at a secret location, and since the number of

copies are limited, patriots are encouraged to make and distribute as many copies of each issue as they can.

Over the next few weeks Gaston became an enthusiastic and efficient distributor of La Libre Belgique. *Several times a month he rode his bicycle to Brussels to pick up the latest issue of the paper, which he would copy and then pass around at school.*

At the same time Gaston continued his tutoring. He had thought of dropping some of his students—in particular, two girls who happened to be the daughters of prominent pro-Nazi politicians. But then it occurred to him that his association with their families might well come in handy as a cover for his resistance activities.

November 11, 1940. Up before dawn to run off the latest issue of *La Libre Belgique.* It's miserable outside: cold and gray, with a biting winter wind blowing wet, frigid air from the north. I heard on the radio a report that students in Paris are planning to commemorate the 1918 armistice by marching to the tomb of the unknown soldier— in open defiance of the German authorities.

After classes I distribute the newspaper to friends I can trust. It's already dark by the time I get home. Pa is sitting at the kitchen table, glaring at my sister. On the table in front of him is a pile of gold tassels.

"Look at what your sister has been up to," he says to me, gesturing angrily at the tassels. "Cutting the braids off the uniforms of German officers."

"I'm not the only one," Simone protests.

Pa slams his hand on the table. "That's no excuse," he snaps.

Simone looks up at me. "You know how crowded the trams are," she says. "The Germans like to push up against the girls and put their hands on us. So we carry razor blades and cut their pretty tassels off."

"And what do you think they'll do if they catch you?" Pa shouts. "They'll do a lot more than put their hands on you!"

He's right, of course. Still, I can't help sneaking a smile at Simone. I admire her spirit.

Pa catches the look and turns on me. "And what have *you* been up to?" he demands. "What's all that ink under your fingernails?"

I look down at my hands. I must've hurried too much this morning. Well, he might as well know.

I pull a copy of *La Libre Belgique* from my briefcase. "I've been printing this," I say. Pa studies the mimeographed newspaper in silence, the color draining from his face.

Finally, he lays the paper on the table. "Why didn't you tell me you were doing this?" he asks.

"I didn't want to put you in danger. It seemed safer for you not to know."

He frowns in thought for a moment, then looks at Simone. "There'll be no more cutting off braids," he tells her sternly. She nods. Then he turns back to me and taps the newspaper. "We'll discuss this later," he says.

After dinner Pa takes me aside and questions me about my work in the underground. Though he pretends to be angry, I can tell he's proud of me. Finally, he shakes his head and sighs. "You should have come to me before," he says. "I know plenty of veterans of the last war who would be glad to help."

I tell him I've been in touch with Commandant Castiaux, who's been lining up friends of his to help get me copies of the latest issue of *La Libre Belgique* from Brussels.

Pa looks at me strangely. Then he shrugs. "I know a broker, a good patriot, who travels to Brussels once a week," he says. "I'm sure he'd be willing to deliver your paper for you."

As winter approached, and the Germans settled into their occupation, food and fuel grew ever scarcer. Gaston began hoarding sugar cubes— not for nourishment, but to drop into the gas tanks of German trucks in order to ruin their engines. Every morning he would walk down to the Grand Place and stroll by the ornate building known as the Kommandatur (which the Wehrmacht was using as its local headquarters) to count the number of disabled vehicles parked out front.

January 3, 1941. I've been thinking a lot about religion lately. I guess I've been impressed by the Castiaux family. Their belief as Protestants seems so generous, so undogmatic. They say grace before every meal, praying not just for family members and friends, but for anyone who might be in trouble or ill health.

One of my tutoring students, a serious young kid named Fonsy, has been telling me about an interesting religion called Sufism. It supposedly teaches that no one religion has a monopoly on truth. I must find out more about this.

January 15, 1941. Home from school after dark to find Pa slumped at the kitchen table, his head in his hands. He tells me a terrible story.

On his way out of the café this evening, his friend Henrik Van den Heuvel heard a woman screaming somewhere down the street. Henrik ran to see what was going on and found two German soldiers attacking her, tearing off her clothes right there on the sidewalk. Henrik knocked one of the soldiers down, then grabbed the other by the collar and began banging his head against a wall. By this time my father and some other friends had come out of the café. The soldier on the ground pulled out a gun and ordered everyone to stay back. Then he put the gun to Henrik's head, and he and the other soldier took him away.

My father immediately ran to get Bervoets, the lawyer, and went with him to the police station. They were too late. The Germans had put Henrik in a cell with three huge soldiers, who broke his arms and then beat him unconscious with iron rods.

Pa stares down at the kitchen table. "They won't let a doctor see him until tomorrow," he says. "By then, Henrik could be dead."

He looks up at me, tears streaming down his cheeks. "There's nothing we can do," he says. "Nothing. For an act of bravery, for defending a woman against these drunken swine, a man is nearly beaten to death. And we stand by, helpless."

It's the first time I've ever seen my father cry. I stand over him, filled with anger but not knowing what to do or say, as he struggles to regain control of his emotions.

He sees the rage in my eyes and shakes his head. "You don't know what the Germans are like," he says. "I know from when I was a boy. My father—your grandfather—refused to work for them when they occupied the country during the last war. They wanted him to build a barracks for them, and he refused. He wouldn't even let his workmen volunteer on their own time. So the soldiers came to our house and dragged him out of a sickbed into the street in the middle of winter. They killed your grandfather because he was a patriot and a brave man. If we fight them, they will kill all of us."

I've never heard this story before. No wonder Pa hates and fears the Germans so much.

January 18, 1941. On the way home from school I pass one of Pa's friends in the Grand Place. He flashes me a "V" sign with his fingers. That's become our symbol in the resistance—that and whistling the first few notes of Beethoven's Fifth Symphony, which the BBC uses to open its news broadcasts.

I signal back, then continue on my way. As I pass the Kommandatur—Wehrmacht officers hurrying in and out, a huge Nazi flag flying overhead—a plan begins to take shape in my mind. I rush home and search through Pa's shop for a bag of lime and a watering can. Then I fill the can with water and pour in enough lime to make a nice whitewash.

After supper I slip back into the workshop and wrap the can of whitewash in coarse brown paper. It's quite heavy, but I manage to carry it back to the Grand Place without anyone noticing me.

It's late, and the square is deserted. I go to a far corner opposite the Kommandatur and untie my package. Then, walking slowly toward the Kommandatur's main entrance, I pour the contents of the watering can onto the cobblestones, drawing a line diagonally across the square. Right now the line is invisible. But when the mixture of lime and water dries, it will turn a thick, chalky white.

Just as I reach the steps of the Kommandatur, a side door opens, and a group of German officers comes out of the building. I flatten myself against a wall, hardly daring to breathe. The officers chat among themselves for a moment. Then—without noticing me—they climb into a car and drive off. As soon as they're gone, I walk to the other corner of the square, pouring out the last of my whitewash in the process. Then I wrap up the watering can and hurry home.

An hour or so later Pa comes bursting into the kitchen, where I'm sitting at the table talking to my mother. "You won't believe this," he says excitedly. "Someone has painted a giant 'V' with whitewash in the square right in front of the Kommandatur!" I don't tell him it was me.

January 19, 1941. In the morning I stroll down to the Grand Place to survey the results of my handiwork. A huge crowd has gathered in front of the Kommandatur, watching as a platoon of German soldiers armed with pails and brooms frantically tries to wash away the enormous "V." Unfortunately for the Germans, the whitewash has seeped into the crevices between the cobblestones, making it impossible to eradicate. Eventually, the authorities close off the square.

January 25, 1941. Another bicycle trip to visit Commandant Castiaux. He introduces me to some friends of his, all (like him) patriotic veterans of the last war. One of them tells a story about hiding a British pilot who was shot down by the Germans. He sheltered the pilot for several weeks until he could make contact with an "evacuation line" that spirited him back to England.

Perhaps if I could make contact with such a line, I too could get to England.

February 10, 1941. I've been reading some books about Sufism that Fonsy lent me. It's amazing—I've never heard of any religion so open, so sensible. Sufism is derived from a Moslem sect in Persia. Instead of looking down on other religions, it sees them as just another way to find God and godliness. If I understand it correctly, a Sufi believes that each person must find his own separate path. To follow dogma or religious leaders who spout dogma, Sufism teaches, is to deny yourself.

As winter turned to spring, the food shortages grew worse. So did morale in the underground, as more and more people were arrested by the Germans and sent off to work camps. Gaston's response was to become even bolder in his efforts on behalf of La Libre Belgique— *running off not just fifty but several hundred copies of each issue and stuffing them into the mailboxes of Nazi sympathizers. As he put it later, "Why shouldn't the traitors know the truth?"*

He also began trying to find someone who might be able to help him get to London. Eventually, a friend at the university told him of an electrician in Brussels who was supposedly in touch with the British and could arrange for passage to England. Gaston was intrigued but wary. He wanted to find out more about the electrician before taking any chances.

April 15, 1941. The university is like a pot that's about to boil over. Demonstrations nearly every day. The pro-Nazis strut around as if they own the place—which, in a way, they do. I suspect the only reason the Germans haven't banned political debate completely is so they can keep tabs on the troublemakers.

Most people are very discouraged. The Germans have massed hundreds of landing boats on the beaches, and many expect the invasion of England to begin any week now. The number of collaborators is growing. Parents are being denounced by their brown-shirt children for being too critical of their superiors, the wonderful "Herrenvolk." With the Germans still advancing on all fronts, more and more people are being seduced by the notion that Europe will soon be unified under the banner of the Third Reich and its "new order." And now posters have gone up announcing that all foreign agents will be shot—along with the entire family of anyone who helps or hides one.

I still refuse to believe that the Nazis will triumph, but in this (as in so many other things) I stand increasingly alone.

May 2, 1941. It's so frustrating. I keep hearing stories about British submarines surfacing just off the coast—or British gliders swooping down at night—to pick up groups of men bound for training in England. But they always involve a friend of a friend. I can never find anyone who has firsthand knowledge of how to make contact with these groups.

I've been asking around about the electrician in Brussels who supposedly knows how to arrange passage to England. According to one story, he's a well-known collaborator; according to another, that's just a cover for his resistance activities.

May 17, 1941. Fonsy takes me to a meeting of anti-Nazi activists at a downtown café. There are about twenty-five of them, mainly extreme leftists. The meeting is supposed to be top secret, and they are hesitant about letting me attend. I'm a bit uneasy myself—partly because they're Communists (Stalin and Hitler *are* allies, after all), partly because I don't know most of them.

They spend most of the meeting discussing the formation of "cells" (small groups of four or five people) and how cell leaders should stay in contact with each other. They also hand out pamphlets that give step-by-step instructions on how to organize a program of widespread sabotage and mass uprisings.

I don't like this sort of thing. It seems to me that, right now at least, sabotage and open revolt are bound to do far more harm than good: as Commandant Castiaux says, it would simply provoke German reprisals on innocent civilians.

May 25, 1941. The Germans have shut down the University of Brussels. I think the only reason they haven't closed Ghent as well is that they're trying to play up to the Flemish-speaking population. Divide and conquer, that's their tactic.

May 30, 1941. A good thing I didn't trust the electrician in Brussels. Turns out he was an agent provocateur in the pay of the Gestapo. Last night he denounced twenty young men who'd fallen for the stories and asked him to help get them to England.

June 2, 1941. More bad news. The Gestapo raided a meeting of an anti-Nazi Communist cell last night. The two lookouts managed to escape, but the four inside (all students) were arrested.

Someone obviously tipped off the Germans. How can people betray their fellow countrymen like that? I just can't understand it.

June 3, 1941. The two students who escaped when the Gestapo broke up their cell yesterday tried to free their captured comrades this morning. A big mistake.

Along with some friends, the students attacked a German staff car carrying the prisoners from the local police station to the Kommandatur. They pushed a cart into the car's path as it approached the Grand Place, then rushed forward and shot the driver. The guards fought them off with machine pistols, wounding two of the students and capturing three.

June 4, 1941. Word at school has it that the Gestapo found a list of resistance contacts at the home of one of the students they arrested yesterday. Now we are all at risk.

I rush home, intending to destroy all evidence of my work with the underground. My mother is waiting for me at the door, scared and anxious. Henri has just been by to report that the Gestapo has my name. I must leave immediately.

I briefly consider going to Brussels, to one of the patriots I've met at Commandant Castiaux's house. But no, time is of the essence, and I'm sure the Gestapo will be watching all the train and bus stations in Flanders.

My mother suggests I go to my Aunt Adele's, on the other side of Ghent. Adele, she says, knows a textile salesman named Lobigny who makes regular trips across the border to France and often carries letters back and forth for the resistance. Perhaps he might be able to help me get out of the country.

We've all known for some time that this moment would come sooner or later. In preparation, my mother's been telling the neighbors that I've been acting crazy, staying out late and disappearing for days at a time, refusing to explain my absences. She'll give the same story to the Gestapo and will also mention that I've been tutoring the daughters of those Nazi politicians. I hope this will confuse things enough to keep my family from getting in any real trouble.

There's no time to pack. I kiss my mother good-bye, then climb on Pa's bicycle and pedal off.

Racing down the Ieperenstraat, I nearly collide with a big gray sedan bearing a black flag on its left front fender and the "SIPO" license plates of the Gestapo. Fortunately, the grim-looking men inside the car take no notice of me.

Aunt Adele lives on a dead-end street crowded with two- and three-story houses. She's surprised and happy to see me, but her mood turns somber when I explain why I've come.

Adele hasn't seen her friend Lobigny for several weeks, but she expects him to show up any day now.

June 5, 1941. Adele has given me a room in her house. I spend most of the day in it, trying to keep my presence a secret from neighbors and passersby. In the evening I venture out into the park for fifteen minutes of exercise.

June 7, 1941. My mother comes to see me, bringing with her a small suitcase packed with my clothing and a few of my mathematics books. She says the Gestapo showed up at our house shortly after I left, demanding to know my whereabouts and threatening to shoot everyone in the family if I wasn't found. I'm evidently considered to be a spy in communication with the enemy—a crime punishable by death. My only hope, the Gestapo men said, is to turn myself in and tell them everything about any contacts I might have had with the underground.

June 9, 1941. Still no word from Lobigny. I don't know how much longer I can stay here at Adele's without someone noticing.

June 10, 1941. How odd it is to realize that I am a fugitive—a wanted man. Too bad I'm an atheist. If I believed in God, I might be able to pray for help.

June 12, 1941. Lobigny finally turns up. As Adele had promised, he's both willing and able to help. I shall be hidden in a load of textiles that he's shipping to France tomorrow. If I'm caught, I can tell the border guards that I jumped aboard the truck without the driver's knowledge.

June 13, 1941. Up before dawn to meet Lobigny's truck on the highway near Adele's house. It's right on time. I hop in the back and burrow beneath the rolls of textiles. For good measure, the driver piles several more bolts of cloth on top of me.

We reach the border at midmorning. From my hiding place, I can hear the driver chatting with the guards. After a cursory inspection—during which they barely glance into the back of the truck—we are waved along.

A few minutes later we're in the French city of Tourcoing. This is still occupied territory, but at least I'm not known here. Following Lobigny's instructions, I jump out of the truck and make my way to the Grand Café, just across from the cathedral in the Grand Place. There I ask for "Charles"—who turns out to be a short, stocky waiter named Charles Blomme.

Blomme tells me to have a cup of coffee and wait for him to get off work. I sit in the café all afternoon, trying to look inconspicuous. Finally, Blomme takes me home to meet his wife, a tiny, heavyset woman with a round, ruddy face and a dazzling smile. Mme. Blomme says she's certain a way will be found to get me to England. She seems delighted to have me as a guest, and insists that I spend the night in her daughter's room. (The daughter, alas, is off visiting relatives.)

The room is small and smells of perfume. I find it difficult to sleep in a strange girl's bed.

June 14, 1941. In the morning Blomme takes me to the home of Robert and Margot Dujardin, a few blocks away. I'm to stay with them until arrangements can be made to transport me to England.

The Dujardins are in their early thirties. Robert is a tapestry salesman, tall and outgoing, with a fondness for Pernod. Margot is short (barely 5'2") and blonde, a bit on the frail side, but very friendly. Both are extremely idealistic and strongly anti-Nazi.

Though the Dujardins are hardly well-off, Margot prepares something of a feast to welcome me: a fine bottle of wine, canned ham, and other delicacies. Over dinner they tell me they're willing to do almost anything to get the Germans out of France and win back their freedom.

June 19, 1941. Still no word on when I'll be able to leave for England. Robert says it could be weeks.

June 23, 1941. Robert takes me to the neighboring town of Roubaix, where a job has been arranged for me at a print shop. He and Margot are very hospitable, but I must earn my keep. I'm put to work on a small hand-fed press producing business forms.

July 15, 1941. I never thought a fugitive's life could be so boring. I wake up every morning hoping for word that the arrangements to get me to England have finally been made. So far nothing.

I've been avoiding the other workers at the print shop, afraid that my heavily accented French will give me away as a foreigner. Fortunately, they seem happy to ignore me. That's not the case with the printer's wife, a buxom woman with long dark hair who wears lots of makeup and fancy clothes. She keeps coming around the shop, looking for excuses to talk to me.

July 18, 1941. Charles Blomme has managed to get a blank identity card from a friend of his who works at City Hall. Using equipment at the print shop, I've filled in my name and description. It's not a very good forgery, but it will do.

July 20, 1941. While the Dujardins go off to church (they've learned to stop inviting me along), I stay at home working. In addition to my mathematics books, I've been studying a copy of *Teach Yourself German,* which I bought a few weeks ago. I've been working at the language steadily, and I think I'm beginning to get the hang of it.

July 25, 1941. This morning at work I'm told to report to the printer's house. He's expecting a load of black-market potatoes, and I'm to wait for them. When the potatoes arrive, I carry them upstairs to a storage area just off the master bedroom. As I pass the bedroom door, a voice calls out my name. I turn. There's the printer's wife, stretched out on the bed, half-undressed. She smiles alluringly and reaches out toward me. I drop the potatoes and run for it.

That's the last straw. I've got to get out of here.

In the evening I send an urgent message to Blomme: I must leave this place as soon as possible.

Chapter Four

On the Run

July 26, 1941. Blomme agrees it's time I moved on. Unfortunately, there's no way I can go directly to England. Instead, I'm to be sent south into Free France.

At the Grand Café, Blomme introduces me to a man called Josef Verquin, an intense red-haired pâté dealer who regularly travels to the nonoccupied zone, often carrying letters for people with friends and relatives on the other side. Verquin tells me the arrangements: on Monday I'm to travel to Mouchard, a small town in the Jura less than a kilometer from the demarcation line. There I'll meet up with a guide who'll lead me and some others across the frontier. After that, I'm to make my way to Toulouse, where Verquin's underground contacts have their headquarters.

July 27, 1941. The Dujardins and I sit up quite late talking about my impending departure and the difficult times that lie ahead for all of us. They've come to regard me as kind of a son, and by the end of the evening we're all in tears. I promise to come back and visit them as soon as I get the chance.

July 28, 1941. By tram to Lille, where I board the Paris train. A few minutes before we're scheduled to leave, a squad of German soldiers comes storming down the aisle, demanding to see everyone's papers. There's no way my phony identity card will stand up to their scrutiny. As the soldiers work their way through the car, I huddle in my seat, wondering if I should try to make a break for it. No, I decide, they'd shoot me before I got ten steps. I'll have to try to bluff my way through.

The soldiers reach my row and order a young French boy sitting next to me to produce his papers. The boy is so frightened he can hardly speak. This is my chance. As he stutters nervously, I grab his papers and hand them to the soldiers, explaining in my rudimentary German that he has a speech impediment. The fact that I speak their language seems to impress the soldiers. They glance at the boy's papers, then move on to the next row without asking to see mine.

A moment later the train lurches into motion and pulls out of the station. I find myself trembling uncontrollably. I can't believe I pulled it off.

We arrive in Paris shortly before noon—my first visit to the City of Light. Fortunately, the train to Mouchard doesn't leave until midafternoon, so I have time to go exploring.

Paris is overwhelming. I wander the streets in awe, gazing up at the landmarks I know so well from books, unable to believe that I'm actually seeing them in the flesh.

There are German soldiers everywhere, and a huge Nazi flag hangs from the Arc de Triomphe. Sitting in a café just off the Champs Elysée, I become convinced that someone is watching me. I look around. All the other patrons seem perfectly innocent. But I can't shake the feeling of being watched. Finally, I go into the men's room and splash my face with cold water. I must remain calm.

The train ride to Mouchard takes the entire afternoon and part of the evening. Following Verquin's instructions, I make my way to an old barn just outside the village. There are a dozen other fugitives hiding in the hayloft: a family of Jews; several young men like myself; and two British pilots, who seem the most self-assured of the lot. Except for the pilots, who chatter incessantly in English, everyone is silent and fearful. I bed down on the dusty straw and try to sleep.

July 29, 1941. Our guide arrives shortly after midnight. He warns us that the German border patrols have strung twine across the paths through the woods. If we're not careful, we'll break the twine as we pass—leaving the Gestapo an easy trail to follow.

It's a clear night with a bright moon. The guide leads us out of the barn and across a freshly plowed field. It's hard to run without stumbling in the furrows. One of the young men in our group is so scared that he unbuckles his trousers to relieve himself.

The guide yells at him to keep moving.

"Can't you wait a second?" someone shouts back. "My God, the boy's lost control of his bowels."

But we *can't* wait a second. With the guide cursing and shouting, we leave the terrified young man behind.

On the far side of the field, we dash across a road and jump into a ditch. We're painfully visible in the bright moonlight. A few yards farther on, we crawl through several rows of barbed wire, then scramble over a railroad track, churning up the gravel of the roadbed as we pass. The noise of the rocks clattering against the rails carries far into the night.

A moment later shots ring out. The Germans guarding the tracks must have heard us. We run for our lives—heading for a thick woods several hundred yards beyond the tracks.

Amazingly, everyone makes it—except for the terrified young man who lost control. I wonder if the shots were for him. I guess I will never know.

The group scatters, dashing heedlessly through the trees, snapping the strings the Germans have stretched across the paths.

I go my own way. After five or six kilometers, I reach another road. I follow it to the outskirts of a village, then hide in a ditch until the sun comes up and the local café opens for breakfast.

The German border patrols are probably already tracing the route our group took through the woods. It's even possible the Gestapo might try to follow some of us into the nonoccupied zone. But I don't care. It's wonderful to breathe free air again, to walk through a town without seeing a single Wehrmacht soldier.

July 30, 1941. By bus to Toulouse. As Verquin instructed, I go straight to the Credit Lyonnais office in the center of town and ask for the representative of the Banque de Bruxelles. A few minutes later a heavyset Belgian appears. He introduces himself as M. Cartigny and asks how he can be of service. When I explain who I am, he frowns and says he knows nothing about the Belgian underground or any clandestine route to England.

Could Verquin have sent me to the wrong man? I tell Cartigny I've been through too much to be brushed off like this. He stares at me intently, then starts to question me about my experiences. After about ten minutes, he is apparently satisfied that I am who I claim to be. I'm to go to the Hotel de la Paix, he says, and wait there for a message.

At the hotel, I'm sent to the third floor, where a ballroom has been converted into a dormitory. The room is hot and smells of unwashed bodies and dirty clothes. Thirty or forty Belgians and a dozen or so Luxembourgers are staying there—all, like me, trying to get to England.

August 2, 1941. After two days of silence, a message from M. Cartigny. It sounds like something out of a boy's adventure novel. I'm to go to a small café called Le Petit Escargot, find the waiter with a mustache, and ask him for Albert.

Le Petit Escargot is on a narrow cobblestone street not far from the Credit Lyonnais office. When I ask the waiter with the mustache for Albert, he tells me to go to the back of the café and take the stairs to the second floor. At the top of the stairs, I enter a small room lit by a single bare bulb. A stern-looking man in civilian clothes is sitting at a table. He fixes me with a penetrating stare, then points to an empty chair across from him.

I sit down. The man introduces himself as a colonel in the Belgian Army Intelligence Service, code name Sabot.

"Gaston Vandermeerssche," I say, offering my hand. Sabot ignores it.

"What is the French name of the street next to the city hall in Ghent?" he asks me abruptly.

"Excuse me?" I reply.

"The street next to the city hall in Ghent," Sabot repeats. "What's the French name?"

"The rue du Paradis," I say, blinking in confusion.

"And how did it get that name?"

I stare at Sabot. He stares back. "Well, because it's so ugly," I finally answer.

He keeps staring at me.

"When the French took over back in the nineteenth century," I continue, "they decided to humiliate the Flemish by giving all the streets French names. And they thought it'd be funny to call this ugly street the rue du Paradis."

Sabot nods, then asks me what courses I've been taking at the university.

"Physics," I start to answer, "and calculus and chemistry and—"

"Give me the names of five of your professors," he interrupts. "Quickly now!"

"Uh, Dekeyser, Verhaeghe, Cnops, Gillis, and Jansen."

Sabot rubs his chin thoughtfully. "All right, Vandermeerssche," he says finally, "why are you here?"

I explain about wanting to go to England to join the Allied armies and help liberate Belgium. Sabot listens patiently, then shakes his head. "Our escape lines are already jammed with refugees and British pilots," he says. "There's no way we can load them up any more."

He hands me a sheet of paper and tells me to read it and then sign the bottom. It's a copy of Belgian military law. I do as Sabot says, and he tells me that I'm now officially in the Belgian army. "I should warn you," he adds, "failure to follow orders in wartime is punishable by death."

What is he talking about? "I'm supposed to be going to England," I protest.

"Don't be stupid," he snaps. "We need you here."

Once again my life is turned upside down. Instead of going to England to join the RAF, I'm to stay here and work for Sabot. My first assignment, he says, will be to establish a courier line over the Pyrenees into Spain. Microfilm and other intelligence material produced by resistance networks in Belgium, Luxembourg, Holland, and France will be shipped via this line to the Belgian consulate in Barcelona. From there, the stuff will be sent on to Lisbon and, ultimately, to Belgian military headquarters in London. The line will also be used to ship goods, information, and money back the other way.

I've got all of three weeks to learn how to act, speak, and look like a Spaniard.

August 4, 1941. I've been trying to think of a place to hide from the Gestapo and Vichy police while I learn Spanish, and I think I've come up with the answer—the chateau at L'Isle Arne, where I spent last summer with the now-defunct 533d. How long ago that seems.

I take the bus from Toulouse to Auch, and then a second bus to Aubiet. From there, it's nearly an hour's walk to L'Isle Arne. The only people at the chateau are Mme. L'Espinasse; her daughter and son-in-law, Mimi and Leon; and the caretaker. They are surprised but also happy to see me. I tell them the cover story I've prepared: that my family has fled to Spain, and I'm trying to rejoin them. Though I have no money to pay them, they agree at once to take me in.

August 11, 1941. I'm working away at my Spanish studies—at it eight or nine hours a day, making and reviewing lists of words until my head swims. Fortunately, the language is a simple one with an uncomplicated grammar, not at all like Dutch or German.

Some friends of Leon's who've spent a lot of time in Spain have been giving me tips on Spanish customs: how to act with strangers, how to order a meal—that sort of thing. I think it will be harder to master these than the language.

For relaxation—and to make my contribution to the dinner pot— I go hunting on the chateau grounds with Mme. L'Espinasse's dog. Today I caught a rabbit.

August 14, 1941. I wake up early, confused and surprised to find the chateau so empty. I'd been dreaming about last summer, when the place was crowded with Belgian refugees. In my dream, Raymonde and I were sitting under a tree, holding hands. Suddenly, I miss her terribly.

Today is my sister's birthday. How is she? I wonder. How much I would like to see her and tell her how sorry I am about all those fights we had in the past year. I've always been annoyed by the fact that she feels entitled to order me around, just because she happens to be one year and four days older than me. After all, she's a female—and anyway, I've been teaching girls much older than her for years. I remember one student of mine, at least four or five years older than me, whom I was tutoring for a very important mathematics exam in Brussels. Boy, what a day that was when she asked me to help her!

Why is it that we make people whom we like—and even love— suffer sometimes?

August 18, 1941. I am twenty years old today. I cannot believe so much has happened to me since my last birthday. What's become of my carefully laid plans—to study math and physics, to go to England? All smashed and scattered. This war plows through our lives like a force of nature—as violent and heedless of what it destroys as a mountain avalanche.

I'm studying Spanish at a little table in the shade of the front porch. From where I sit, I can see Mme. L'Espinasse feeding her geese. That's just how I feel as I make myself memorize a hundred new words a day—like one of those geese they force-feed to produce foie gras.

August 21, 1941. A day trip into Toulouse to see M. Cartigny at the Banque de Bruxelles. I've written a letter to my family—just to let them know that I'm alive and well. Cartigny says it will be sent to them via the same underground line that brought me to Toulouse. To speed a reply, I tell my mother in the letter to write to me directly at the Chateau L'Isle Arne.

I'm tempted to write to Raymonde, but I wouldn't know what to say.

September 1, 1941. Word from home! My mother has received my letter and has written back to tell me everyone is fine. How I miss them all!

Madame L'Espinasse tells me that the letter from my mother aroused the mailman's curiosity. Who is this Belgian receiving mail at the chateau? he wanted to know. How long has he been here? These Frenchmen, always curious, always poking their noses into other people's business.

September 2, 1941. I'm sitting at the big table in the kitchen, studying my Spanish, when Mimi bursts into the room, shouting that the gendarmes from the village are surrounding the chateau. I dash out the back door and, like a rabbit, dive into the densest thicket I can find.

Carefully, I crawl through the underbrush, slipping past the ring of policemen closing in on the chateau. Then I make my way to a nearby farm run by relatives of Mme. L'Espinasse. They agree to hide me for the night.

How did the police know I was at L'Isle Arne? I can't believe any of Leon's friends would have told anyone.

September 3, 1941. With the help of Mme. L'Espinasse's relatives, I sneak into Auch and get on the bus to Toulouse. Back in the city, I hole up in the Hotel de la Paix and send word to Sabot. I still can't figure out what could have gone wrong.

September 5, 1941. I meet with Sabot at Le Petit Escargot. He listens to the story of my escape, nodding silently, then asks who outside the chateau might have known where I was.

"No one," I reply, "except for you and my parents."

Sabot blinks in surprise. "What do you mean, your parents?" he asks.

I explain about telling my mother to write to me directly at the chateau. Sabot's face darkens, then he explodes with anger. Evidently, I've violated a basic rule of security. By telling my family where I was, I put the entire organization at risk.

I sit there, shaken and ashamed. Then, abruptly, Sabot asks how my Spanish is going.

I stare at him dumbly. Sabot is always changing the subject without warning.

"Your Spanish," he repeats. "Have you learned enough to try a trip across the border?"

I'm not sure I have. But I can't tell him that. Instead, I take a deep breath and assure him I'm ready.

Sabot hands me a large envelope sealed with wax. "Your first delivery," he says. I'm to go to Osseja, a village in the Pyrenees, where a member of the underground named Rene runs a small hotel.

Rene will arrange for a guide (Sabot calls him a *passeur d'homme*) to lead me through the mountains into Spain. Once across the border, I'm to deliver the sealed envelope to the Belgian consulate in Barcelona. There I'll be given hard currency and documents to bring back to a variety of places (Sabot calls them "letter boxes") stretching from Toulouse all the way north to Brussels.

Sabot adds that I'll need a cover name and asks if I have any preferences.

I think for a moment. Unbidden, an image of a slender blonde girl swims into my mind. "How about Raymond?" I say.

September 10, 1941. My first mission as a courier. I take the train from Toulouse to Bourg-Madame, a small town in the foothills of the Pyrenees. There, at La Tour de Carol, I transfer to the cog railway that runs up the mountain to Osseja.

I arrive in Osseja late in the afternoon. The village is surrounded by huge peaks, nearly fifteen hundred meters above sea level. My destination, the Hotel Calvet, is just across the Grand Place from the railway station.

Rene is waiting for me. He is short and skinny, with dark hair and a deep tan. He tells me that a *passeur d'homme* named Diego— a reliable guide from an old mountain family—has agreed to take me across the Pyrenees tonight. According to Rene, the mountain people have been smugglers for generations. They have no allegiance to any government, and the war hasn't made them one bit more patriotic. They simply regard it as yet another opportunity to turn a profit.

Our destination will be a safe house just outside the Spanish village of Ribas. Ribas is only thirty kilometers from here as the crow flies. Trouble is, we're not crows. On foot, Rene says, the trip will take us at least twelve hours.

Diego turns up just before dusk. "The rules are simple," he says. "You keep at least twenty meters behind me, but no further than thirty. If you get lost or fall behind, you're on your own. If we run into any trouble, it's every man for himself."

We set off just as the sun is going down. In the long twilight shadows, the village seems lonely and deserted.

Diego leads me across a rocky meadow, then breaks into a trot and disappears into a dense thicket. I follow. We jog through the forest for a kilometer or two, climbing steadily upward. Eventually, we emerge onto a goat path high above the village. Osseja sits at one end of a valley. The goat path leads to a pass through the mountains at the other end.

It takes us several hours to reach the pass. The night is clear, lit by a brilliant full moon. We must be nearly three thousand meters up, but still the Pyrenees tower over us, their snow-covered peaks glowing eerily in the moonlight. The cold mountain wind makes me shiver in my sweaty clothes. I can't believe I'm doing this.

We climb and climb. Each time we reach a crest, an even taller mountain looms in front of us. Do they go on forever?

After what seems like an eternity of climbing, we arrive at the top of a second pass. Below us stretches a huge snowfield. We tramp through it for nearly an hour. Finally, Diego beckons to me. "Spain," he says, pointing to the valley floor far below. In the distance, at the bottom of the valley, I can see a lonely house with a red roof. Diego follows my gaze and nods. That's where we're headed.

I wish we could stop and rest, but we must reach the safe house before the sun comes up.

Soon we are climbing down through a blackened forest, devastated by a recent fire. I thought it would be easier going down than up, but it's not. My feet keep slipping, and it's a struggle to stay erect. The sweet, acrid smell of damp burnt wood fills my nostrils. Ashes cover my wet clothes. In the unreal light of the moon, the ruined trees look like grotesque, petrified monsters. It's as if we're exploring another world. There are no signs of life—no birds, plants, or animals. Only the eerie whistling of the wind and the snapping of charred branches under our feet break the silence. This could be the land of the dead.

We reach the safe house just before dawn. A tall Spaniard with dark, deep-set eyes is there waiting for us. Diego speaks to him in a dialect I don't understand, then leads me upstairs to a small bedroom. The bed is hard and very narrow, but I don't care. I'm asleep the moment my head hits the pillow.

September 11, 1941. I take an ancient, battered bus from Ribas to Ripoll, where I board the train to Barcelona. We arrive at the Estacion Barcelona Vilanova shortly after noon.

What an amazing city this is! I wander wide-eyed through the Arcuida de la Meridiana, crowded with peddlers pushing their carts and old women in black dresses haggling over produce. Then I make my way through the Parque de la Ciudatela to the harbor district and the waterfront. The wharves are crowded with ships flying the flags of what seem like dozens of nations. Barcelona is an open port, and trade is clearly booming.

Eventually, I find my way to the Belgian consulate on the Calle Arajon. Following Sabot's instructions, I take the ancient, ornate elevator to the third floor and ring the bell on an unmarked door at the end of the hall. A moment later an eye peers out at me through a peephole.

"My name is Raymond," I say. "Sabot sent me."

A middle-aged woman opens the door. Behind her, I can see a small waiting room with three chairs along one wall and a small desk in front of the only window. She motions me to take a seat, then disappears into an inner office. Before long a youngish-looking man comes out and introduces himself as an attaché. I hand him the envelope Sabot gave me. He breaks the seal and looks inside. The envelope is filled with rolls of microfilm. From here, another courier (a Belgian code-named Ramon) will take them to Lisbon, where they'll be put on a plane to England. For the time being, at least, my job is done.

September 12, 1941. After a pleasant night at the consulate (the attaché treated me to the biggest meal I've had in months), I'm eager to see more of Barcelona and try out my Spanish. I find a bar near the waterfront and order a drink and a plate of *mejas*— small white clams. At least that's what I try to order. Instead, the waiter brings me *aceitunas*—hard green olives.

Rather than confuse things even further, I decide to accept the *aceitunas* without protest. I've seen how the Spanish eat them— stabbing the olives with toothpicks, then popping them into their mouths. As it turns out, it's not as easy as it looks. My first stab sends the olive skidding off my plate. I cringe in embarrassment, praying that no one's noticed.

I try a second time. Once again, the olive goes flying.

By now, I'm convinced the whole world is watching me. Carefully, I take aim at a third olive. Sabot says a secret agent must always make sure to be inconspicuous. If I miss this time, I don't know what I'll do.

I raise my toothpick, let fly and . . .

Perfect—I spear the olive solidly and pop it in my mouth. Nothing to it.

September 13, 1941. To the consulate in the morning to pick up a pile of bulky envelopes wrapped in waxy, waterproof paper—my cargo for my trip back across the Pyrenees. The largest of the envelopes contains a thick wad of cash—thirty thousand American dollars to be delivered to the chief of Groupe Zéro, an important intelligence network based in Brussels. The man to whom I am to give the money is a banker code-named Aristide.

By the end of the day I'm back in Ribas, knocking on the door of the safe house. The concierge—the tall Spaniard who greeted Diego and me the other day—has been expecting me. He's not very talkative, but I get the impression that he fought on the Republican side during the civil war here. While I rest in a bedroom, he goes out to find me a *passeur d'homme*.

September 14, 1941. The return trip over the mountains is exhausting. I'm told that most people take two or three days to make the crossing. To do it in less than twelve hours, as our schedule demands, we have to trot most of the way.

We cross the border around midnight, reaching Osseja just as the sun is coming up. At the Hotel Calvet, Rene gives me a room to rest in. After a few hours of sleep, I take the cog railway down to Bourg-Madame, where I board the train to Toulouse. I am expected in Brussels in three days and have half a dozen stops to make along the way. No time to waste.

September 18, 1941. I'm in Brussels, staying with Commandant Castiaux. It's my first time back in Belgium since I fled three months ago, and it's strange, even a little painful, to be here. So close to home, yet I don't dare try to contact my family.

The commandant was astonished when I appeared on his doorstep, having assumed that I'd long since made it to England. "How did you get here?" he asked. "Did they drop you by parachute?"

I quickly brought him up to date on my activities. The last few days have been a blur of letter boxes and safe houses, dropping off documents, collecting rolls of microfilm. I've also been looking out for potential recruits. As Sabot says, the underground needs all the help it can get—people to maintain letter boxes, run safe houses, and keep an eye on enemy rail and troop movements.

Fortunately, there are a lot of patriots out there—ordinary people who are willing, even eager, to do what they can. I've already enlisted a number of friends: among them, the Dujardins and Charles Blomme. Castiaux agrees at once to join the group.

September 19, 1941. Over breakfast, Commandant Castiaux suggests that he become a kind of recruiting officer for me. As the head of the Belgian veterans' organization, he knows plenty of patriots who would love an opportunity to work with the resistance. I explain to him the importance of referring to me only by my code name, Raymond. None of the people he recruits should know my real identity—or the real identity of any other agent in the network. That way, if any of them are caught by the Gestapo (or turn out to be traitors), the rest of us will still be safe.

Later Castiaux introduces me to Jean Van Cauwenberghe, the mechanic who takes care of his car. Van Cauwenberghe is a dedicated anti-Nazi who often hides downed Allied pilots in a small room above his garage. His brother-in-law, Gaston Garreyn, owns a nearby dairy shop, which Commander Castiaux feels would make an excellent letter box for my fledgling network.

The letter-box system is really quite ingenious—a wonderful example of applied logic. Entrance to the letter box, which could be anything from a hardware store to someone's apartment (or, as in this case, a dairy shop), is controlled by a code and a willed action. The code is a password that the agent must give to be admitted to the letter box. An agent who forgets his password—or an unauthorized person (such as a Gestapo man) who doesn't have one—will simply be turned away.

The willed action is a signal set by the person running the letter box to indicate that the coast is clear and the letter box is safe to enter. If the letter box happens to be a butcher shop, for example, the signal might be a particular arrangement of meat in the window; if it's an apartment, it might be a newspaper left on the stairway. With Garreyn, I work out a system involving the position of milk bottles in a rack by the door.

The beauty of this system is that if an agent gets in trouble, he doesn't have to do anything to warn off his colleagues. If, say, he's forced by the Gestapo to enter a suspected letter box, all he has to do is *not* give his individual password, and the people running the letter box will act as if they don't know him. Similarly, a person running a letter box who thinks he's being watched by the authorities can simply sit tight; the fact that he's not set the all-clear signal will alert his agents that something's wrong.

Security is maintained by keeping all letter boxes independent of each other, with no more than six agents per letter box. In addition, each agent has his own unique password and all-clear signal. That way, if an agent is arrested, he can't compromise anyone's safety but his own.

In the afternoon I go to see Aristide to deliver the money I carried back from Barcelona for Groupe Zéro. One of the founders of *La Libre Belgique,* Aristide is an official of the Banque de Bruxelles with an office at the bank's headquarters on the Rue Royale. His real name is Albert Hachez.

I arrive at the bank—a large nineteenth-century building fronted by a courtyard and surrounded by ornate iron gates—shortly after noon. Two armed guards are standing watch at the entrance. I walk past them into the lobby and hand the receptionist a note. A few minutes later, word comes back that Aristide will meet me in a basement office in another building owned by the bank about four blocks away.

Aristide turns out to be a heavyset man, just a little taller than me but at least twice my weight. Though only in his twenties himself, he seems surprised at how young I am. Nonetheless, he treats me with respect—especially after I hand him the thirty thousand American dollars I was given in Barcelona.

He has some documents for me to take back across the Pyrenees. "This is important work you're doing," he says to me as I leave. "I hope you're up to it."

Until the spring of 1940, when the Germans invaded Belgium, Gaston had never been more than fifty kilometers from home. Now, as a courier for the Belgian resistance, he began crisscrossing the Continent regularly, journeying back and forth between Brussels and Barcelona nearly every week. Over the next two months, he crossed the Pyrenees on foot a half dozen times.

Gaston also continued his recruiting efforts, building a sizable network to support the operations of what came to be known as the Raymond-Ramon line. By mid-November, Gaston could count on the help of nearly a hundred agents in three countries. Some provided the names and addresses of trustworthy people who believed in the Allied cause, people willing and able to provide shelter for couriers or Allied pilots who had been shot down. Others, with access to government offices, supplied ration coupons for food and clothing, blank identity cards, and other vital documents. And everyone passed along whatever information they could glean about the attitude and behavior of local politicians and police—were they patriots or willing collaborators?—as well as the workings of the Deuxième Bureau and the other secret-police organizations.

Sabot, aware that the larger a network got the easier it would be to infiltrate, worried that Gaston's organization might be growing too fast.

Chapter Five

In the Pyrenees

November 14, 1941. I'm in Bordeaux staying with a relative of Commander Castiaux, a physician named Freyche who runs the local civil-defense organization. Like Castiaux, Dr. Freyche is a real patriot, eager to do what he can to help the underground. He has nearly fifty young people working for him—most of whom feel the same way. I suggest he put them to work keeping an eye on the harbor, which is filled with German warships. He agrees immediately.

Because of my connection with Castiaux, Freyche is no problem to recruit. I wish it were always so easy. Many prospective agents are skeptical of my bona fides—mainly because of my age. (I suppose I *am* a bit young to be doing this sort of work.) What I do in such cases is ask the prospective agent to give me a code word or phrase, anything he cares to make up, which I then pass on to London through our radio operators in Roubaix and Brussels. When skeptics hear their code phrase broadcast back at them over the BBC, their doubts about me usually disappear.

November 15, 1941. To a modest little house on the outskirts of Bordeaux to see Lucien, a *cheminot,* or railroad worker, whom Dr. Freyche says can sneak me aboard a train that will take me to Toulouse in the nonoccupied zone. Many of the *cheminots* are Communists

with no love for the Nazis, and most are more than willing to help
the resistance.

Lucien is a short but powerfully built man in his mid-forties. Somehow he seems to have expected me. He asks if I can wait until
tomorrow night to get on a train, and when I tell him I can, he
leads me to a wardrobe from which he begins pulling out a huge
collection of old work clothes, which he asks me to try on. A half
hour or so later, after trying on what seems like a hundred different
outfits, Lucien finally nods with satisfaction. When I look in the
mirror, I can hardly recognize myself.

Lucien completes my transformation into a railroad worker by
giving me an old hat. It keeps slipping down over my eyes, so he
stuffs paper into the crown. To complete the outfit, he gives me a
railway man's lantern, which he teaches me to light, and a battered
old leather pouch, which I sling over my shoulder.

November 16, 1941. In the evening, I dress up in the work clothes
Lucien gave me and, with my leather pouch over one shoulder and
my lantern in my other hand, I leave Dr. Freyche's house for the
railroad station. Even though I look older than my age, I'm afraid
that anyone who takes more than a glance at me will see that my
face is too young looking for the clothes I'm wearing.

As there's nothing I can do about that, I square my shoulders
and walk straight to the entrance that Lucien told me to use. I
have no idea what to expect. Will the German guards ask to see
my papers? Will they expect me to speak to them? My heart pounding,
I lower my head and stare at the ground as I shuffle past the guards.
To my vast relief, the Germans wave me on through without a word—
as if they were used to seeing me come in every evening.

Following Lucien's instructions, I walk to the end of the platform,
then jump down onto the tracks. Stopping behind an empty passenger
car, I light my lantern. It takes a long time because my hands are
shaking. When I finally get it lit, I trot down the line to the switching
yard, where hundreds of boxcars—some standing by themselves,
some in strings, some already made up into freight trains—are scattered about seemingly at random. It's as if some giant child had
gotten bored with his toys and just thrown them into a heap.

After wandering about for ten minutes or so, I manage to find the freight train with the numbers Lucien gave me. I walk down the train, looking for the boxcar Lucien told me to board. There should be a series of slots in its side, its sliding doors should be open, and its number should begin with the letters "UF."

Finding the car turns out to be a lot easier than getting into it. Though its doors are open as promised, its floor is extremely high, and there is nothing to grab onto. Finally, I manage to fling myself aboard. Just as Lucien promised, there is a large dog box built into the far-left corner of the car. It's about one meter square, the sort of thing used to transport people's pets. Using the special railroad "key" Lucien gave me—an L-shaped piece of steel with one triangular end and one square end—I open the dog box and peer inside. It's very dark in there. No way to see if there are any rodents or spiders waiting for me.

With a sigh, I toss my pouch and lantern in first, then climb into the box to see how much room I'll have. With the door closed, my chin is between my knees, and the lantern is poking me in the back. I can see that this is not going to be a pleasure ride.

According to Lucien, the trip to Toulouse will take between five and six hours. We'll be in the occupied zone for the first four hours or so. Then, just before we cross into the nonoccupied zone, the train will stop so the Germans can inspect it.

Sitting in the dog box, even with the door closed, I can hear a startling variety of strange noises and voices outside. I never realized how busy a railroad yard can be at night. There are the whistles— long and short, high and low—so many of them. And the banging and rattling of the boxcars as they are coupled and uncoupled, pushed and pulled around the yard.

After a while, the banging and rattling get louder as if they're coming closer. Suddenly, something smashes into the car I'm in, knocking it backward a few feet. I'm thrown forward, slamming my head against the door to the dog box. The car stops, then is bumped again, then a series of bumps, each one progressively less intense than the last. Finally, the car begins to roll forward, at first quite slowly, then rapidly gaining in speed.

I decide to open the dog box and stretch my legs. The night air is cold and crisp and quickly chills me to the bone. I peek out the sliding door. We're moving along at quite a clip now. It's amazing how quickly we leave the city behind.

After about three hours, the train starts to slow, and I decide to get back into the dog box. I spend the next half hour—which seems more like six to seven hours—shifting and fidgeting, trying without success to find a comfortable position. It's not easy, given the fact that I'm determined to keep one hand firmly on the railroad key in order to prevent it from slipping out of the keyhole when the Germans inspect the train at the border.

Finally, amid the squeal of brakes, the train comes to a stop. From outside, I can hear a variety of voices—some French, some German—yelling a variety of things. My heart begins to pound. I hear several pairs of heavy boots—soldiers, no question about it— marching quite near. Then nothing. The soldiers must be inspecting the car in front of mine.

Sure enough, a moment later I hear some more heavy bootsteps. Then I see some lights flashing through the tiny cracks in the outside wall of the car. The lights move from the front of the dog box to the back. It sounds as if there are at least three soldiers walking toward my car.

The soldiers come closer and closer, until they can't be standing more than two feet from where I'm hiding. Then they climb into the car and walk around. I can't believe how my heart is pounding.

One soldier walks straight over to the dog box and kicks the door. My heart nearly jumps out of my body. Is it possible for a person to faint from fear? If so, I don't know how I'm still conscious.

I wait for another kick, but it never comes. A few moments later, I hear the soldiers walk back to the door and jump to the ground. Then I hear them climb aboard the car behind mine.

It's all over. Still, I sit tight for another half hour, trying not to move a muscle until I feel the train get under way again.

The next few hours are blessedly uneventful. We arrive in Toulouse just as the sun is coming up.

November 20, 1941. Back in Brussels, staying in the room above Jean Van Cauwenberghe's garage. I've established this place as a kind of Brussels headquarters for myself. It's not fair—or safe—to always be taking advantage of Commandant Castiaux's hospitality.

I'm feeling terribly homesick. I wish I knew how my parents and sister are doing. Unfortunately, Castiaux has no news.

I really do miss my mother. Of all my family, she is the one who understands me the best. It amazes me, when I think about it, how patient she is, how she is always sacrificing herself for others. Her whole life has been characterized by self-sacrifice. It began when she was a young girl and had to give up her dream of being a singer. She had such a wonderful voice. They were always asking her to sing at family gatherings, and she enjoyed performing as much as the relatives enjoyed listening. But her father was convinced that performers lived in a world of sin, and so she was not allowed to pursue singing as a career.

Instead, she became a grade-school teacher—mainly because that's what her father and two older sisters did.

Mother also learned to cope with hardship. When I was young, the family was pretty well-off. Business at Pa's carpentry-and-cabinet-making shop was so good that we could afford a country cottage in a beautiful spot on the river Leie about fifteen kilometers from Ghent. Pa would go fishing there, and I learned to sail and canoe. We'd also spend a month's vacation every year on the North Sea in an apartment by the beach at St. Idesbald.

But then the depression hit, and several of Pa's biggest customers—mainly movie theatres, for which he made wooden seats—went bankrupt. As a result, both the country cottage and the beach place had to go—along with most other luxuries. Meat and butter became increasingly scarce in our house. Occasionally, hunger became a reality for us.

For solace, Pa turned to drinking. Often, he would come home late at night and start a fight with Mother. Neither Simone nor I knew what to do. We began to be afraid of Pa, while our love for our mother deepened.

I always had mixed feelings about Simone. When I was younger, I used to admire my big sister for all the things she could do that I couldn't. But as I got older, it became increasingly clear that I was a lot smarter than she was. I was always number one in my class at school, I had all those scholarships and grants from the "Fund for Gifted Children," and from the age of eleven I was tutoring other students for money. Indeed, by the time I was fourteen, I was spending practically more time tutoring other kids than going to class myself. My mathematics professor would even send me some of his own private students if he had too many to handle or considered them "hopeless."

My policy as a tutor was simple: I would tell my students that if they didn't pass the exam for which I was preparing them, they didn't have to pay me. Needless to say, this made me quite popular— though the fact is, never once did I have to return a student's tuition. In any event, I think my success as a tutor bothered Simone. It certainly contributed to the friction between us over the last few years.

How could I have let such stupid resentments come between us? It's times like this that make me realize how much I love my family, and how little of that love I've been able to express to them. I guess I'm not very good at communicating my feelings. How I wish I could have spoken up when I had the chance.

In the afternoon to Biez to see Raymonde. She is happy to see me, but she doesn't want to know what I am doing. I suppose that's just as well.

November 22, 1941. A summons from Sabot. He's got special orders for me. On my next trip through the Pyrenees, I'm to escort a Belgian cabinet minister who is on his way to join the government-in-exile in London. Evidently the big boys feel it would be best if a native Belgian accompanied the minister through the mountains. I'm to pick him up in Monaco, where he's been holed up ever since the Germans overran Belgium. That means crossing an extra border, but I don't mind. After all the borders I've been across these past few months, what's one more?

November 26, 1941. Monte Carlo is so pretty you'd never know there was a war on. The minister is staying in a large and elegant house—almost a small chateau, really—on a posh street. Whoever owns it must be very rich.

A uniformed maid answers my knock on the door. She stares at me coldly until I tell her that I'm Raymond come to collect his package. Then she nods and invites me in. A few minutes later the minister appears. He's elderly, but tall and powerful looking. I'm pretty sure I saw his picture in the newspapers before the war, but I can't for the life of me remember which government department he runs.

He peppers me with questions: When exactly will I come for him? How long will each leg of the trip take? What are the mountains like?

I tell him that we'll meet at the restaurant in La Tour de Carol the day after tomorrow. How he gets there is his own business. From there, we'll travel in the usual way—that is, no direct contact: he stays at least ten meters behind me at all times. If anything goes wrong, he's to return to Monaco and await further instructions.

He seems quite emotional—even scared—about the whole thing. It's as if he finds me somehow intimidating. Isn't that crazy?

November 28, 1941. Our rendezvous in La Tour de Carol is bizarre, to say the least. To my relief, the minister arrives without incident. The owner of the restaurant here is an agent of mine. (He was recommended to me by Rene, who manages the Hotel Calvet in Osseja.) He leads the minister and me to a private room in the back, where we can wait undisturbed until it's time to catch the cog railway up to Osseja.

The minister is very nervous and agitated, and he paces about like an expectant father. Then, without warning, he bursts into tears and falls to his knees in front of me. Gasping incoherently, he begs me to help him, to spare him, to protect him.

I don't know what to say. Sharply, I yell at him to pull himself together. We're supposed to be leaving in a few minutes, but we can't go anywhere until he calms down. In the state he's in, the border police would be onto us in a minute.

Eventually, the minister regains his composure. We leave the restaurant fifteen minutes behind schedule, nearly missing the train to Osseja.

The trip across the mountains is a nightmare. The minister is no outdoorsman, and he makes me stop every ten minutes so he can catch his breath. As a result, it's long past daybreak when we finally cross the border into Spain. Fortunately, there aren't any patrols about, and we make it to the safe house without incident.

December 8, 1941. Amazing news from America. The Japanese attacked an American naval base in Hawaii yesterday. As a result, the United States has declared war on both Japan and Germany. It was the Americans who made the difference in the 1914–18 war. I am certain it will be the same this time. Now things will begin to change, and fast!

December 15, 1941. Back in Toulouse, staying tonight at the home of a Belgian army adjutant named Adolphe Manet. Under cover as a salesman, Manet runs a letter box and safe house for us. He's a tall, slender man with slicked-back dark hair and a perpetually gloomy expression. Sabot doesn't trust him. As he sees it, Manet lives a bit too well. He always has money in his pocket and spends an inordinate amount of time in cafés and restaurants. He claims to have made a pile wheeling and dealing on the black market, but it's equally possible that he's on the Gestapo's payroll.

Whatever his game, Manet keeps me up well past midnight, peppering me with questions about my work. He doesn't exactly press for details, but every time I try to change the subject, he comes back with a new question.

December 31, 1941. At Aristide's invitation, I celebrate New Year's Eve in Brussels with him and his assistant Claire. They take me to a fancy nightclub with an elaborate floor show. As I watch the beautiful show girls in their skimpy costumes, I begin to realize how strictly my parents raised me. I've never thought about it before, but I really don't know very much about life.

As the evening wears on, Claire begins to play footsie with me under the table, rubbing her bare foot against my leg, first around the knee, then higher and higher. It makes me both tremendously excited and tremendously embarrassed. I'm blushing furiously, convinced the entire restaurant is watching me. Yet neither Claire nor Aristide seems to notice a thing.

I feel dizzy. When is the show going to end? I want to get out of here, but I don't dare stand up—I have a terrible erection, and I know everyone will see it.

We wind up staying until the club closes in the wee hours of the morning. Aristide asks me to see Claire home. It's the last thing I want to do, but he insists—with all the German soldiers around, he says, it isn't safe to let her go alone.

When we get to her apartment, Claire asks me in for a nightcap. I'm too scared to take her up on the invitation. I don't know how I manage to say good night to her, but somehow I do.

The new year brought with it a new determination on the part of the Germans to root out the underground once and for all. In the crackdown that followed, the Gestapo began stopping cars, trains, buses—anyone could be pulled aside and checked at any moment. It was dangerous enough crossing frontiers at the best of times; with border stations more heavily manned, Gaston found himself playing a weekly game of hide and seek with mountain patrols that winter, flirting with capture every time he crossed the Pyrenees.

As winter rolled into spring, Gaston neared the end of his useful life span as a courier. Sabot reckoned that an agent could safely handle the same assignment for no more than six months; after that, his luck was bound to run out. By April, Gaston had been running the Raymond-Ramon line for seven months.

April 15, 1942. Back in Brussels, staying with the Castiauxs again. How I wish I could go to Ghent and see my own family. That, of course, is out of the question.

April 20, 1942. As a result of the Gestapo's stepped-up interest, I decide to take a different route back to Toulouse. I make my way to Bordeaux, where I go to see Lucien, my *cheminot* compatriot. Once again, Lucien outfits me with the right clothes and helps me sneak into the rail yard, where I hop aboard a flatbed car piled high with huge cannon barrels. According to Lucien, the cannon barrels are being shipped to a secret factory somewhere in the south.

The barrels are covered by a heavy canvas sheet. Perfect, I think— not only will it hide me, it should also keep me warm. I climb under the canvas and stretch out between the barrels while the car is hitched to a long train. An hour or so later, the train lurches into motion and we're off.

It turns out to be hideously cold on the car. The icy metal literally sucks the heat out of my body. I have to move every few minutes to keep from freezing. The train rattles its way south through the night, but sleep is out of the question.

Around dawn we pull into a yard just outside of Toulouse. I'd like to find out exactly where the cannon barrels are headed, but I'm too cold and hungry and exhausted to go on any further. Instead, I jump off the car and find a *cheminot*, who lends me some clothing and a false identity card.

Help like this makes me wonder how long the resistance would last if we didn't have the support of so many ordinary people. These are not the best of times. There is so much fear, and for good reason. Every city and town seems to be plastered with those huge Gestapo posters warning that anyone who helps "foreign agents" or "spies" will be shot without delay—along with their entire family. No wonder it is getting harder and harder to find people willing to provide us with food and lodging. But even though there have been more and more arrests, more hostages taken and shot, more agents and downed pilots caught and killed, we continue. With the overwhelming majority of the people on our side, how can anyone doubt that eventually we will win?

April 24, 1942. I arrive at Adolphe Manet's apartment to find his wife in a panic. Adolphe was arrested and badly beaten last night by agents of the Deuxième Bureau, the Vichy secret police. He's currently in bed recuperating. Madame Manet doesn't say it outright, but I get the feeling she thinks the underground might have set Adolphe up as a kind of test—to see if he'd talk in custody. She could well be right.

April 25, 1942. Another meeting with Sabot at Le Petit Escargot. I've been running the Pyrenees line so long now that he feels it may simply be a matter of time before the Gestapo catches up with me. As a result, he wants me to train a backup, who could replace me in case I'm captured or killed.

My backup is to be Ramon, the courier who runs the Barcelona-Lisbon line. I'm to meet him in a safe house in Barcelona, then take him through the mountains so he can learn my route and contact points.

April 28, 1942. The wind from the mountains is cold and wet in my face as I step from the train at Bourg-Madame. I have two hours to kill before the cog railway leaves for Osseja, so I wander down the cobblestone streets to a café called Chez Blanche and sit down to wait.

Two old men are gossiping at a table nearby. "The mountains are filled with police," I hear one of them say. "They found two bodies near a goat path last night, throats cut. No jewelry or money, but good clothes. Probably Jews trying to escape to England."

I stare into my café au lait and try to look inconspicuous. Though I'm dressed in mountain clothes, I'm still a stranger here, and the mountain people are suspicious of strangers. When I finally board the cog railway, the other passengers stare at me with unconcealed curiosity.

At the Hotel Calvet, Rene pours two glasses of Pernod and leads me to a table near the front window, where we can watch the street while we talk. He says the Jews who were murdered in the mountains last night were supposedly carrying a fortune in gold and jewels. Most likely, they were killed and robbed by the guide they'd hired to take them across the Pyrenees to Spain.

I tell Rene about my problems with the Gestapo, and how I need a *passeur d'homme* who can show me a passage through the mountains that I haven't used before. Rene suggests a smuggler called Garcia. "From an old mountain family," he says. "Proud people. And honorable, I think."

Garcia appears at the hotel just after sunset. He is small and dark with a hawk nose, wearing a leather jacket and a beret. A cigarette droops from his lip. "My price is five thousand pesetas," he says by way of greeting. "You can pay me now."

Garcia's route through the mountains is a good one, but there's still plenty of snow on the ground, and the going is slow. We reach the border around midnight. The snow is very thick here, and Garcia plunges down the mountainside, slipping and sliding like a child on a Sunday outing.

It's a struggle to keep up. I don't like it. Garcia's going too fast, making too much noise.

Just above the tree line, Garcia stumbles and falls into a drift, triggering a small avalanche that crashes through the forest below us. The sound echoes across the valley.

A few minutes later, as we're approaching the trees, we hear a shout: "Halt! Stop before I shoot!"

A carabinero is standing in the path below us, his rifle raised to his shoulder. Slowly, Garcia and I put up our hands.

The carabinero lowers his rifle and starts toward us. Suddenly, Garcia makes a break for it, jumping off the path and scrambling down the mountainside, leaping from rock to rock like a goat. I race after him.

A shot rings out, shattering the early-morning quiet. Garcia and I keep running. Then another shot explodes from the woods above us. Garcia cries out and drops to his knees.

I rush to his side and pull him under a ledge. He's taken a bullet in the back, just below the left shoulder. Gasping in pain, he tells me to go on without him. "Take the path down to the river," he says, "then follow it into Planolas. From there, you can find your way to Ribas."

"We'll go together," I protest. "I'll help you."

Garcia shakes his head. "If you want to help, go to the cobbler's shop in Planolas and get my brother, Manuel. Tell him I'll be in the cave under the big pine. He'll know what to do. Now go!"

Above us, I can hear the carabinero crashing through the underbrush, looking for us. I run down the path without looking back.

April 29, 1942. I reach Planolas just before dawn. It doesn't take me long to find Manuel's house. I rouse him from his bed and tell him what has happened. He stares up at the mountains for a long moment, then offers to take me to Ribas in his wagon.

"What about your brother?" I ask.

Manuel shrugs. There's nothing he can do for his brother until nightfall, he says. Not with the mountains swarming with carabineros.

I can't believe how callous he is. "But your brother's been shot," I say. "He could be dying."

"If my brother didn't feel he could wait," he replies coldly, "he wouldn't have sent you to me. He'd have gone to the cave to die alone."

While I hide in the woodshed, Manuel hitches an ox to a heavy farm wagon. Then he helps me into the wagon and covers me with a pile of animal skins. The stench is nearly unbearable, but I stay buried beneath the skins as we rumble down the bumpy mountain road. Manuel pretends not to notice when I jump off the wagon at the outskirts of Ribas.

April 30, 1942. A day of rest and recovery in Ribas, then on to Barcelona. I make my way to the Calle Arajon, where I find a black Citroen parked directly in front of the consulate. A sallow-faced man—obviously Gestapo—is sitting behind the wheel, reading a newspaper.

I walk quickly past the car and trot up the steps into the consulate. As I wait for the elevator, my back to the entrance, I can hear the Gestapo man getting out of his car. What is taking the elevator so long? I can't let the German get a good look at my face.

The elevator arrives just as he enters the lobby. I jump in and slam the gate shut.

I get off on the third floor and go straight to the attaché's office to get the address of the safe house where I'm to meet Ramon. It turns out to be in the suburbs, about five kilometers from here.

Before I go anywhere, I've got to lose the Gestapo man parked out front. I think for a moment, then walk down to the second floor and push the button to summon the elevator. When I hear it start up, I take the stairs to the lobby. The Gestapo man is just outside the entrance, leaning against his car. As soon as he sees me, I turn and race back up to the second floor, where I jump into the waiting elevator. While the Gestapo man clatters up the stairs after me, I ride down to the ground floor and hurry out of the building.

At the entrance to an alley a half block away, I glance back at the consulate—just in time to see the Gestapo man come running out the front door, looking around in confusion.

Satisfied that I've lost him, I follow the alley to a narrow street that opens into a small square, where little boys play soccer with rag balls, and old men sit on benches in the sunshine feeding the pigeons. I stop for a few minutes in a darkened doorway, looking around to make sure no one else is tailing me. Then I take a winding route through the old part of Barcelona toward the hills that surround the city.

Eventually, I reach a steep suburban street lined with high stone walls, broken only by a few wrought-iron gates, through which I can see small gardens. Near the top of the street I find the address I'm looking for—number 874. I ring the bell. An old woman appears at the gate, squinting at me quizzically, her face creasing into a thousand wrinkles.

I give her the password, and she lets me in. Muttering to herself in a Catalan dialect I can't understand, she leads me around the side of the house, down a narrow set of stairs and into a dark cellar filled with wine casks and cobwebs. She lights a candle and walks to the end of the long cellar, where she pulls aside an old tapestry and raps firmly on a hidden door. "Raymond e acqui," she announces.

A metal bolt slides open, and the door swings ajar, revealing a comfortable room with a large fireplace at one end and a table and chairs at the other. A short, stocky man with wavy blond hair, bushy eyebrows, and a mustache to match is seated at the table. He rises as I enter and shakes my hand warmly. "Welcome, Raymond," he says. "We've been waiting for you."

I look at him blankly. "I am Charlotte," he says. My jaw drops. Charlotte is the overall chief of Belgian military intelligence. His real name is William Ugeux. Along with Albert Hachez (who later adopted the code name "Aristide"), Ugeux was one of the principals of *La Libre Belgique*. He also founded the Groupe Zéro intelligence network, which Aristide took over when Charlotte became overall chief of intelligence for the Belgian government-in-exile.

"I've heard a lot about you," Charlotte says to me. "You're much younger than I expected."

Another man is standing in the corner. He is tall and slender with black, curly hair and a thin, hawkish nose. Charlotte introduces him as Paul Levy, the voice of Radio Brussels. Levy greets me warmly, explaining that he came over the Pyrenees last week and is waiting for a safe passage to England, where he will resume broadcasting for the underground.

I can't believe how friendly he and Charlotte are. How many times I have heard Levy's deep, rich voice on the radio; how many times I have heard other agents talk about Charlotte with a respect that borders on awe. Now here we all are together—the famous personality; the legendary intelligence chief; and me, a little kid from Flanders—talking as if we're old friends. I feel proud and embarrassed at the same time.

After dinner the three of us sit in companionable silence on a second-floor balcony overlooking the city, drinking amontillado and eating small *mejas* (clams) and black olives. After a while Levy starts talking about Barcelona. He calls it "a brawny, working city that smells of fish and sweat and wine and spices." His booming voice fills the night. "During the civil war, the people here denounced the state *and* burned the churches," he laughs. "There's an explosive power here. A sense of violence and anarchy that you can feel. The war only makes it more intense."

He picks up the bottle and pours himself another glass, which he knocks back in silence. The three of us sit there, not speaking, each lost in our private thoughts, for another hour or so. Then, as if by some unspoken agreement, we rise as one and go off to our beds.

May 1, 1942. Levy leaves for Portugal after breakfast. An hour later Charlotte sets off too. He doesn't tell me where he's headed, and I don't ask. He does, however, leave a present for me: I had admired the blue silk shirt he was wearing yesterday. Now it's mine.

May 7, 1942. Still no word from Ramon. I'm going mad with boredom, but Charlotte's orders were clear. I'm not to leave the house until Ramon arrives.

May 16, 1942. A message from the consulate. Ramon is in Barcelona!

He arrives at the safe house late in the afternoon, a dark and wiry man, about ten years older than me, with a condescending manner. "So you're the famous Raymond," he says when the old lady introduces us. "You're not what I expected. You look French, but you speak like a boy from Flanders."

"And you," I reply, "you look like a Spaniard, but you talk like a Walloon."

Ramon looks me over—not in a friendly way, more like a fighter sizing up his opponent. "Are you sure you're ready to teach me your route?" he asks.

"Are you sure you're ready to learn it?" I retort. The mountains, I tell him angrily, are no place for amateurs. If the ice and snow don't get you, there are border guards on both sides who will.

Ramon doesn't seem impressed. "Don't worry about me," he says. "I'm ready to go right now."

This doesn't bode well. I don't like the idea of crossing the Pyrenees with someone I don't trust.

May 18, 1942. Traveling separately for safety, Ramon and I take the 10:00 A.M. train from Barcelona to Puigcerda. It's very crowded, and I wind up standing in a corridor filled with peasant families. The smell of cheap tobacco and unwashed bodies is overpowering.

We get off the train on the Spanish side of the border, a few stops before Puigcerda, and walk the rest of the way to Ribas. It's late in the afternoon by the time we arrive. The sky is overcast, and the Pyrenees are barely visible.

With Ramon following a discreet distance behind, I hike out of the village, then turn off the road onto a footpath that runs across a sloping meadow. At the far end of the meadow, a woodcutter's cottage sits at the edge of a dense forest. I knock on the back door and tell the woodcutter we're looking for a *passeur d'homme* to take us across the Pyrenees tonight.

"Impossible," he says. "The snow is melting too fast. Come back in two or three weeks."

He starts to close the door.

"I'll pay seven thousand pesetas," I say.

That seems to change his mind. He tells us to wait by the house while he sees if he can find someone in the village.

Ramon doesn't like it. "Are you sure he can be trusted?" he asks me as the woodcutter trots off. "Maybe he's trying to stall us so he can inform the police."

I tell him not to worry. These people don't take sides, but they hate the Germans as much as we do.

The woodcutter returns an hour later. He is alone.

"I can't help you," he mutters. "Come back in two weeks."

I tell him I'll pay ten thousand pesetas.

The woodcutter shakes his head. "I spoke to a man who was up in the mountains yesterday," he says. "The snow was so soft and wet it took him two hours to climb a single kilometer."

I raise my offer to twelve thousand pesetas. "But that's my limit," I warn him.

The woodcutter laughs sourly and spits on the ground. "You can pay ten times more and no one will go," he says. "A dead man does not need money."

He retreats into his house, slamming the door behind him. Angrily, I lead Ramon back across the meadow. The sun has set, but the moon is nearly full.

Ramon turns his collar up against the cold night air. "It's a good thing we're going to wait," he says. "It sounds really dangerous."

"We're not waiting," I tell him. "We will go without a guide. Tonight."

He stares at me in surprise.

Once again, I tell him not to worry. I've been through these mountains fifteen times. If I don't know my way by now, I never will.

Ramon buys some supplies in the village—a bag of biscuits, a handful of sugar lumps, a few chocolate bars, and two liters of wine. Then we set off.

I lead him up a rocky path along the side of the valley. "We take this path to the top of the ridge and then follow the crest," I explain. "Watch for three huts near the end of the valley. When we reach them, we follow the ridge to the right."

Setting a brisk pace, we wind our way steadily upward, always keeping to the high ground. The mountain streams are swollen with runoff from the melting snow, and small lakes have formed in many of the glens.

After several hours of climbing, we reach the crest of a high ridge. A few hundred yards ahead of us, I can just make out three small shapes moving through a pine grove. I motion for Ramon to get down. We crouch there, out of sight, our hearts pounding.

Suddenly, three mountain goats dart out from the trees and bound across a clearing. I stand up and give Ramon the all-clear signal.

"It's a good sign," I tell him. "It means there's no border patrol around here."

We climb on. We should be above the snow line by now. But we're not. I can't believe so much has melted.

An hour or so later, as we're reaching the end of the second valley, I hear the sound of running water. I look up. The face of the ridge we're approaching glistens like silver in the moonlight. It's water from the snowfields above, sheeting down in a torrent.

"It's beautiful," Ramon says. "Look at it sparkle!"

I'm not so impressed. The melting snow has turned the ridge face into one wide river. And we're going to have to walk across it.

We stop to rest at the edge of the torrent, eating our biscuits and drinking the last of our wine. I tell Ramon to fill his wineskin with water. When we reach the high passes, there won't be any streams. We'll be surrounded by snow, but we won't be able to eat enough to quench our thirst.

After a few minutes we resume our climb, stumbling and falling in the cold water rushing down the slope. The next ridge, a few hundred meters higher up, is even worse. It's covered with a thick layer of snow and ice. With each step we break through the layers, the ragged edges of the ice scraping our legs as our feet plunge into puddles of freezing water hidden below.

We climb for four painful hours, until we're completely drenched and .exhausted. I've long since lost track of all the landmarks and am guiding us strictly by instinct.

Finally, at the top of a particularly long ridge, I collapse onto a rock ledge, waiting for Ramon to catch up. Wearily, I stare out across a broad expanse of snow. In the distance, the great black shapes of the Pyrenees rise high into the sky, their summits lost in the clouds. Ramon clambers up behind me and follows my gaze. "Oh, my God," he whispers hoarsely. "Do we still have so far to go?"

I point across the valley at the eastern horizon. Dawn will be breaking in less than half an hour. We should be on the other side of the border by now. If a patrol sees us, we've had it.

Ramon is near tears. "I beg you," he says. "I've got to rest for a while. My feet are frozen. They hurt so much I can't stand it."

I tell him to take off his boots. He looks at me strangely, then complies. I put his right foot between my thighs and hold it there while I massage his calf. Then I switch to his other leg. Slowly, the strain seems to leave his face.

May 19, 1942. We push on just after dawn—nearly blinded by the glare of the sunlight reflecting off the snow. Around noon, just as I'm climbing onto an icy ledge, my hand slips, and I go sliding back down the slope headfirst. Ramon grabs after me, but there's nothing to hold onto, and we both tumble head over heels in the snow for several hundred meters before we can dig in our heels and skid to a halt.

"Are you okay?" Ramon gasps in his native French.

"Yeah," I answer in Flemish. "I think so."

For security's sake, we should be speaking only Spanish on this side of the border. But we're too tired to care. Slowly, we struggle to our feet and make our way back up the slope to the rock ledge, where we sprawl in the sun and drink the last of the water in our wineskins.

Ramon's lips and cheeks are cracked and raw. "Come on," I say, "we've still got a long way to go."

He lifts an arm to stop me. "I can't go another step," he whispers in a small, trembling voice. "We're out of food. We're out of water. We're finished."

I squat down beside him. "You've never been through these mountains before," I tell him. "I have. Believe me, you're only finished when you give up."

He shakes his head wearily.

I decide to take a different tack. "A lot of people are depending on us. You can stay here and die if you want, but you'll do it alone. I'm going on."

I stand up. Ramon looks up at me for a long moment, then starts to get to his feet. He's not ready to die—at least not just yet.

We climb steadily through the afternoon, growing more numb and exhausted with every step. To keep myself from slipping into delirium, I begin shouting encouragement at Ramon. Soon my words are barely more than grunts and shrieks. Finally, they're just bursts of air from my aching lungs.

Every hour we stop to warm each other's feet between our thighs. We're too tired to talk, too tired even to think.

Soon the sun goes down. I have no idea where we are, but I daren't let Ramon know. We plunge ahead blindly, falling and getting up, plodding erect and crawling on our hands and knees.

Around midnight we stop to rest. Our immediate surroundings seem completely foreign to me, though the peaks in the distance look vaguely familiar. To our left, an immense rock wall towers straight up to the sky. Where is the pass?

"We must be near the spine of the mountains—the border," I tell Ramon. I point to a mountain directly ahead of us. "We'll go around that peak and then down."

We climb for several hours around the base of the peak, eventually reaching the top of a ridge that slopes away from the mountain. We collapse wearily onto a large, flat rock overlooking a steeply sloping snowfield. While Ramon warms my feet, I stare out at it. Off to the right, I can see the first fingers of the rising sun. Then it hits me. The snowfield slopes down to the north. We've crossed the border! We've made it!

"There!" I cry hoarsely, pointing to the valley below. "France!"

I try to stand up, but my legs are too weak. Gathering up all my remaining strength, I push myself off the rock and go sliding feetfirst down the slope. The top layer of snow is frozen solid, and I speed down the snowfield like a human toboggan. After several hundred meters, I see two large rocks below me. Twisting my body and kicking, I slalom to my left and zigzag down the slope for another five hundred meters or so. Finally, I dig in my heels and stop near a small ledge in the snow.

Behind me, I can see Ramon following my example. I crawl to the edge of the ledge, then kick off again. This time I slide at breakneck speed for more than a kilometer. I twist to my right to avoid some trees and find myself hurtling down an even-steeper slope, completely out of control. Suddenly, with a huge splash, I plunge into a deep pool of swirling, icy water.

For a moment I'm completely stunned. Then I fight my way to the surface and crawl out onto the hardened snow, gasping for breath. A moment later Ramon crashes into the pool. I help him onto the bank. We lay there, shivering uncontrollably in painful spasms.

Finally, I struggle to my hands and knees. In the dawn light, I can see a pine forest less than a kilometer away. "Come on," I gasp to Ramon. "Fire. Now."

We stumble toward the forest, dripping wet and freezing. I don't know where my energy is coming from. Perhaps this is what they mean by the survival instinct.

Reaching the trees, we fall to our knees and frantically scrape together a pile of branches. But what shall we use for kindling? I think for a moment, then reach into my knapsack and pull out a brick-shaped package wrapped in oilcloth.

Ramon stares at me wide-eyed as I rip open the oilcloth, revealing a thick wad of American thousand-dollar bills. I'm meant to distribute the money to the network chiefs throughout Europe. The funds are so crucial to the resistance effort that I'd rather die than lose even one of the bills. Fortunately, I think I have a way to both save our lives and still get all the money to where it is needed. With trembling hands, I carefully tear off a tiny corner from each of several dozen bills. Soon I've got a small pile of green-and-white paper in my hand.

Ramon digs into his pocket and produces a cigarette lighter. He flicks it and gets a spark, but no flame. The wick is dry—no fuel.

"Take it apart," I suggest. "Maybe some fuel is left inside."

Ramon unscrews the bottom of the lighter with his thumbnail. Then, using a small twig, he pries the cotton wadding out of the fuel compartment and spreads it among the torn-up money in my hand.

He holds the lighter over my palm and looks at me solemnly. "If you don't catch this spark," he says to me, "I'll kill you."

He flicks the lighter. A small spark jumps from the flint, but nothing catches. He flicks the lighter again and again—until his thumb and forefinger are raw and bloody, and he has to use the side of his hand.

Finally, a spark hits the cotton—and it bursts into flame.

"Mon Dieu!" Ramon cries. "A miracle!"

I nudge one of the small scraps of money toward the tiny flame and blow on it lightly. It catches. Carefully, I add more paper. Ramon adds a twig or two. The flames grow. Fortunately, my hands are too numb to feel any pain.

When the twigs are burning, I place the little fire onto the bed of branches we've prepared on the ground. In a few moments, a healthy fire is crackling away.

"We're going to make it!" I shout, hugging Ramon. Tears are streaming down his face.

We kneel over the fire, feeding it with larger and larger branches, until we have quite a blaze going. If there are any border patrols in the vicinity, they'll have no trouble finding us. But who cares? We're going to live! We lay down next to the fire to dry ourselves off and soon fall asleep.

May 20, 1942. I'm awakened by a sharp pain in my legs. Opening my eyes, I see that our fire has burned down and is smoking rather badly. So are my trousers. I pull my legs away from the fire and sit up. Ramon's pants are smoldering too.

"Wake up!" I shout, shaking him. "You're on fire!"

He opens his eyes, confused, then cries out in pain and jumps to his feet. "Where are we?" he asks.

I have no idea. What I do know is that by now the border patrol must have seen the smoke from our fire.

Ramon and I drown the fire with clumps of snow, then head off, following a path through the woods. The pain from the burns on our legs helps keep us awake, but it also slows us down. Finally, around noon, we reach a large clearing overlooking a valley—in which we can see the red tile-and-slate roofs of a French village.

We start down a logging trail. Soon we meet up with a peasant walking alongside an ox cart. It turns out we're just fifteen kilometers from Osseja.

We stumble into the Hotel Calvet in Osseja just before dusk. Rene is shocked to see us. The border police and the gendarmes spotted our fire, he says, and have been looking all over for us. He offers us food and salve for our burns, but we can't stay with him—it's too dangerous.

Instead, we're to take the train to Montpellier. Sabot is waiting for us there at a safe house in Sète.

We arrive at the safe house around 8:00 P.M.—only to discover the place dark and the front door ajar. While Ramon waits across the street, I enter the house. It's a mess—furniture overturned, papers scattered everywhere. Obviously raided by the Vichy police.

Quickly, I back out of the house and hurry down the street. Ramon follows. A few blocks away, I duck into an alley and grab him as he walks by. "We've got to split up," I tell him. "If they've caught Sabot, there's no telling how many others may be arrested."

I give him the address of a safe house in Narbonne. We shake hands and wish each other luck, then leave the alley in opposite directions.

I take the train north to Chalon-sur-Saone, where an agent of mine—an engineer named Marcel Orset—sneaks me across the border into occupied France. Orset manages a number of stone quarries in the unoccupied zone and, as a result, has a special pass that allows him to cross the border almost at will. In order to take advantage of this freedom, he has modified his Peugeot, turning it into an ingenious smuggler's vehicle.

What Orset has done is cut out the plate behind the car's backseat, creating a small double-walled compartment in which a person could hide. The compartment is so tiny that Orset has to fold my legs and arms in a precise way to get me to fit. Once I'm in, he points to a little piece of rope attached to the seat back right in front of my nose and tells me to hang onto it for all I'm worth, just in case one of the German border guards tries to pull the backseat out.

According to Orset, the Gestapo has raided a number of safe houses in France and Belgium, and dozens of agents have been arrested. (Fortunately, Sabot doesn't seem to have been among them.) If any of them crack under interrogation—and some are bound to—the entire organization could be at risk.

The raids evidently began after the Gestapo stopped a small van that regularly carried several thousand copies of *La Libre Belgique* from Brussels, where it is printed, to Lille. (Most likely, the Germans had been tipped off by a suspicious neighbor who noticed the van leaving the print shop early every Saturday morning.) When the SS men searched the driver, they found a small notebook containing the addresses of some twenty safe houses where stacks of *La Libre Belgique* were to be dropped off. Several Gestapo cars were immediately dispatched to each of the addresses, and a lot of arrests were made. Fortunately, one of the safe-house keepers managed to escape through a back door when the Germans came calling. He came straight to Orset and told him of the crackdown.

The driver, meanwhile, was taken to the Gestapo headquarters on the Avenue Louise in Brussels, where he was thrown into a holding cell with a number of other people, one of whom he recognized as a doctor who had been arrested several times for voicing his strong patriotic feelings in front of German soldiers. The driver was able to give the doctor a brief account of what had happened, begging him to somehow smuggle out word to the underground that the safe houses had been compromised. By some miracle, the doctor was able to get word out the same day, alerting what remained of the network to lie low.

Once across the frontier, I board the night train to Paris. It's very crowded, and I have to stand the entire way. Though my legs throb with pain from my burns, it's a struggle to stay awake.

Given what Orset has told me, I have no idea what to expect in Tourcoing and Brussels. Have my contacts been compromised by the raids? What about the Castiaux family and Gaston Garreyn?

May 21, 1942. I stumble off the train in Paris at daybreak, exhausted and nearly delirious, my legs stiff with pain and fatigue. My destination is an old hotel that we use as a safe house in a seedy part of the seventeenth arrondissement. As I near it, my sixth sense tells me I'm being followed. I trot down the short flight of steps that leads to a small courtyard in front of the hotel, then duck into an alcove. A moment later I spot a man I'm certain I saw earlier near the train station. He is hard to miss: He's a real thug with virtually no neck, hardly any transition at all between head and shoulders. He's standing across the street, looking around suspiciously. The moment he sees me watching him, he turns away.

I walk out of the courtyard and head slowly down the street toward a metro stop. When I hear a train coming, I dash down the stairs to the station, waiting at the bottom to see if the man will follow. He does.

This is not the first time I've had to shake a tail. With all the news from Orset, I'm frightened—perhaps more than I need to be. I must keep cool. I can't afford to make any mistakes.

Trying to act calm, I wait on the platform as the train discharges its passengers. Then, just as it is about to leave, I jump aboard the first car. My tail leaps for the third car, barely managing to squeeze through the closing doors.

Fortunately, the train is jammed. Hiding in the crowd, I pull my dark-blue beret and a pair of thick glasses from my pocket. I put them on and remove my jacket. I've never been so glad that I've made a habit of always carrying my beret and glasses. I can't count the times I've used that beret in the Pyrenees to conceal my blonde hair or cover my freezing ears. The nice thing about the beret is that it folds up so conveniently, and there are so many different ways you can wear it.

When we reach the Gare du Nord, I get off the train. So does my tail, but he doesn't seem to recognize me in my disguise. At one point, he looks straight at me, then moves on. Can he be faking? There's only one way to find out. I walk out of the station. As I do, another young man, with blonde hair like mine and a jacket similar to the one I was wearing, draws his attention. It's too good to be true. The last I see of my tail, he is running down the street after the man who looks like me.

My worries were clearly justified. I must leave Paris at once. Rather than trust any of the safe houses, I will go to the Dujardins in Tourcoing. The fact that I'm the only one who ever stays there gives me confidence that it—and they—are probably still secure.

I go back into the Gare du Nord and catch the next train to Lille. Exhausted, I spend virtually the entire trip pinching myself (almost to the point of drawing blood) to stay awake.

In Lille, I board the tram to Tourcoing and make my way to the Dujardins' apartment. Despite the Gestapo's well-publicized threat to shoot anyone caught hiding an agent, they don't hesitate to take me in.

Seven boys leave Ghent for Toulouse. Gaston is second from the right.

On four bicycles.

Commandant Albert Castiaux in his office. L'Isle Arne. 1940

Front row: M. Desobry, Gaston, M. Lamboray, Marcel, Commandant Castiaux. Behind them, the cooks.

Leaving, August 13.

The Castiaux and Desobry families. Two cars for nineteen people.

The kitchen staff; L'Isle Arne. Castiaux first on left; Gaston, top right.

Waiting in line for food.

The concierge of the château, Mme LesPinasse

Commandant Castiaux's wife and family: Jeannine, Violette, Liliane, Eveline, May, René and Paul

Gaston's father before the war. 1937.

Gaston's father after his release from the concentration camp at Mathausen in 1945.

Gaston Vandermeerssche in 1952; director of the center for electron microscopy, University of Ghent.

Leopold, forty years later (Pierre de Stexhe).

After forty years, meeting a Dutch agent (WIM) who had been condemned to die with Rinus.

The Castiaux's home in Uccle. Secret meeting place during the war.

In memory of the 54 agents in the intelligence service of The Netherlands who died for our freedom. Englandspiel 1942–1944.

Chapter Six

Questions for London

May 23, 1942. Two days of rest at the Dujardins' is not nearly enough, but I must move on. I've got to get to Brussels, where I can find out just how badly we've been hurt. The news is not encouraging. Robert has been monitoring the BBC and reports hearing coded messages disguised as personal communications—"L'église de St. Bernard est brûlée," "Le père de Susanne est gravement malade," "Georges est au dentiste"—indicating there have been Gestapo raids throughout France, Belgium, and Luxembourg.

May 25, 1942. I take the "Mongy," the streetcar that runs from Tourcoing to Lille to Roubaix. There, I head straight for Le Panier d'Or, a café we use as a meeting place. As soon as I step in the door, Madame Blondin, the wife of the owner, greets me with a big smile and asks me what I will have to drink. This is her signal that the coast is clear, that to her knowledge there are no Germans in the café, only local patrons.

I sit down and order a cup of coffee. When she brings it to me, she whispers, "I will call Raymonde right away. She should be here within half an hour." This is not my Raymonde, but the daughter of a customs agent. The Germans have replaced very few of the customs agents who work along the French-Belgian border, and many of the holdovers are patriots. Raymonde and her father live in a house situated in no-man's-land, the narrow strip of territory between the French and Belgian frontiers, and they have special papers that allow them to go back and forth across the border at will. As a result of years of guarding against smugglers and black marketeers, they know the best places to cross without being observed. They also know which guards are friendly, and which are bound to cause trouble. And they are more than willing to share their knowledge with underground couriers like myself.

Several times a day, Raymonde drops in at a café in Roubaix to see if there are any couriers who need help getting across. If there are, she tells them when and where to meet her. Depending which guards are on duty, she sometimes escorts the couriers openly, walking with them hand in hand right in front of the German guardhouse. At other times, she waits until after sunset and then leads the couriers along a little path that begins in a friend's backyard and runs two hundred yards across the frontier to a backyard on the other side.

Today she gets me into Belgium by the more private route. Once across, I take the train to Brussels, where I hole up at Commandant Castiaux's house and send word to Aristide that I want to see him.

May 27, 1942. I meet with Aristide at a small restaurant at the Porte Louise not far from his office at the Banque de Bruxelles. Aristide likes this place because it is close to several tramlines—an important consideration if one ever finds it necessary to make a hasty getaway. Also, the owners are good patriots and friends of his.

According to Aristide, the situation is pretty dismal. Not only has the Gestapo offensive hurt us badly, but the incompetence of the boys in London has reached outrageous proportions. Despite our repeated warnings, they continue to drop agents in France and Belgium dressed in British clothing, smoking British cigarettes, and carrying currency that the Germans called in months ago.

He has doubts—and I share them—about whether any of the information we've been sending to London has been getting to the right people. Neither of us has any clear idea of just how Allied intelligence is organized in London, but there must be several competing services. Just as there's tremendous infighting between the various German intelligence and police organizations—the Wehrmacht, the SS, the SD, the Abwehr, and SIPO (not to mention the Gestapo, which everyone hates and fears)—so too the Allies must have their own intraservice rivalries.

In any case, Aristide says that I'm to cut off contact with all sabotage groups. He also wants me to go to the train station this afternoon to meet with Marc, who runs the Luc-Marc intelligence network. Over the past few weeks, Luc-Marc has been decimated by the Germans, and poor Marc is half crazy with fear and concern for his people.

After lunch I get on a streetcar heading for the Gare du Nord, where Marc is supposed to be waiting for me. A block or so from the station, I spot a Gestapo roadblock up ahead. Dozens of SS troops are forcing people to line up against walls and storefronts, inspecting their papers, and arresting anyone who even looks suspicious. Without waiting for the streetcar to stop, I jump off and circle around the commotion on foot.

Marc is standing in a crowd in front of the railroad station, watching from a distance as the soldiers go about their business. He is nervous and sweating, and when he speaks he's barely coherent. I drag him off to the Palace Hotel, sit him down in the restaurant, and try to settle his nerves. Panicking won't help anyone, I tell him. We've got to be cooler than ever, assess the damage the Gestapo has done to our networks, and try to rebuild.

Eventually, Marc calms down, and we start comparing notes. By combining what he's heard from his remaining couriers and what information I picked up in Chalon, Tourcoing, and Lille, we begin to get a rough idea of who's been arrested and who has not. We're even able to make some guesses about who may have talked under interrogation. As a result, we are able to come to some tentative decisions about rearranging some of the courier lines and interchanging some of the safe houses. By the end of our conversation, Marc seems to have regained his sense of humor—a good sign.

Whoever said that no news is good news didn't know what he was talking about. I am finding that some news, even if it's bad, is infinitely preferable to operating in a vacuum. When you don't know anything, you tend to fear the worst (at least I do). Knowledge—even just a little—makes things easier to take. You can make plans. You don't have to just sit there in the dark, wondering.

June 1, 1942. To a dry-cleaning shop near Le Pont du Germoir, not far from the university quarter, to meet once again with Marc. The shop, run by a patriotic old woman called Madame Angele, is one of Marc's letter boxes. The security system he uses is different from the one I employ in my letter boxes and safe houses. Instead of depending on passive signals (such as the arrangement of milk bottles in a window) to indicate whether or not it is safe to enter, you actually have to go into the shop and speak to Madame Angele in order to be recognized as "good" or "bad."

I don't much like this system. It strikes me as too unsafe, for the agents as well as for Madame Angele. Indeed, I said as much to Marc at our last meeting.

Before entering Madame Angele's shop, I look around to see if anyone is following me. The street is empty. As I step inside, a chime rings, summoning Madame Angele from the back of the shop.

"You have something to pick up?" she asks me.

Marc has briefed me on how to answer. "Yes," I reply. "I'm here to pick up Marc's blue jacket, which he brought in last Friday."

Madame Angele smiles and nods. "Go right in," she says softly. "Marc is waiting for you."

She points to the door behind the counter. I walk through into the back room, where I find Marc sitting at a fine-looking mahogany table arranging hundreds of sheets of paper—some with typing on them, others covered with handwriting—into several piles.

"Salut, Raymond," Marc says, rising from his chair to greet me. "Come on in, and let's get to work. We have lots to do."

Marc explains that each pile of papers represents a different sector (or team of agents). The individual sheets contain the names and addresses of individual agents. What we have to do is go through each sheet, assign each name and address a code number, record the code number on another sheet, cut the names and addresses off the original sheet, then place the paper in the appropriate pile. After this is done, we will reassemble and renumber the lot for a photographer, who will make microfilms of everything. The microfilms, grouped in order of priority ("Super Urgent," "Urgent," and "Regular"), will then be assembled into packages of ten to sixteen rolls. Each of these packages is about the size and shape of a one-pound pack of butter—which is why underground couriers refer to packages of microfilm as "packs of butter." (Similarly, a package of money, of the sort that I often pick up in Barcelona, carry across the Pyrenees, and deliver to Brussels, is known as a "pack of sugar.")

As Marc and I work, we continue the discussion we began at our last meeting on the state of our networks, trying to figure out which courier lines have been penetrated and which have not, which of our surviving people need to be evacuated immediately and which can merely be put on temporary inactive status. Finally, we draw up plans to reroute our microfilm traffic around the penetrated lines. It looks as if somewhere between twenty and twenty-five of our people have been arrested. Both of us have the distinct impression that a double agent is at work somewhere. For some reason, Marc is counting on me to find out who the double agent is.

Sorting Marc's papers takes several hours. When we're done, we cram everything into Marc's large briefcase. We both feel reassured. The Gestapo may be on our backs, but we're still in business.

We agree that I will leave first. Marc wants to stay for another hour or so attending to some personal papers. I open the door a crack and peek into the shop. Except for Madame Angele it is empty. I nod to Marc, then step out into the shop. Madame Angele smiles at me. I bid her au revoir, then walk out the front door into the street like an ordinary customer. As I do, three well-dressed men appear on my left and enter the shop. As they pass me, I hear them speaking to each other in German. Gestapo agents? They must be. Why else would three men go into a dry-cleaning shop together?

There's nothing I can do but hurry off down the street.

Gaston was right. The men were Gestapo. A few days later, Marc told him what had happened. Sitting in the back room of the dry-cleaning shop, Marc had heard the Germans come in and begin to shout at Madame Angele, demanding to know where her husband was. Marc immediately grabbed the briefcase containing his papers, jumped onto the table, and scrambled out the window and down an alley. He got away cleanly. Madame Angele did not. She was arrested by the Gestapo and sent to an extermination camp in Germany.

For the next six weeks Gaston was on the run constantly, traveling back and forth between Brussels and Toulouse with virtually no rest. With fewer and fewer safe houses available to him, he spent most of his nights sleeping in railway stations, literally under the noses of patrolling German gendarmes.

Though the pace was exhausting and the pressure relentless, Gaston's courier network remained in business. Indeed, it continued to grow. In the Toulouse area alone, he had nearly thirty agents maintaining letter boxes, manning safe houses, and gathering information. With the help of the redoubtable Dr. Freyche, he widened his operations in Bordeaux, recruiting a number of people who lived and worked in the port area. Eventually, these recruits were able to provide Gaston with copies of shipyard work schedules as well as maps detailing the strength and position of the German antiaircraft emplacements that ringed the port.

Through Charles Blomme's friend Verquin, the pâté dealer, Gaston was also beginning to establish contacts in and around Carbonne. One such contact turned out to be a godsend. A clerk in the police identity-card office, he could provide Gaston and his agents with all the new ID cards they wanted. He was also in charge of collecting the old ID cards when local residents died. Since these cards had belonged to real people, they were even more valuable to Gaston's couriers than new ones, for which fake identities had to be invented.

Another new recruit was in charge of issuing ration coupons for food in the area. With his help, Gaston and his network were able to obtain dozens of extra coupons for meat, bread, sugar, and other necessary staples.

In Tourcoing, meanwhile, Charles Blomme recruited a man who worked in a large gravel-and-cement yard. While the owners of the yard made a fortune collaborating with the Germans, their employee aided the Allies by providing Blomme with valuable information, which Gaston and his couriers passed along to London: tonnage and destinations of virtually every day's cement, brick, and steel shipments. With this kind of data, Allied intelligence analysts could pinpoint just where along the coast the Germans were constructing new bunkers.

At the same time, from his agents in cafés throughout France and Belgium, Gaston was compiling a fairly complete list of German uniform insignia—information crucial to keeping track of troop movements. His agents were even able to check the insignia worn inside

soldiers' caps or in the linings of their overcoats. This kind of detailed
observation was supplemented by the work of agents who supervised
railroad crossings in several little villages. By taking note of the
markings on the tanks, trucks, and other heavy vehicles that the
Wehrmacht often moved by rail, they helped keep tabs on how the
Germans were deploying their forces.

July 22, 1942. I make my regular delivery of money and papers to
Aristide, then bicycle out to visit Raymonde in Biez. To my astonishment, Raymonde's father practically slams the door in my face, shouting at me to go away and not come back. "Do you know what the
Germans do to people who take in agents?" he yells in a high-pitched
voice. "They shoot them! I won't have you endangering my family's
safety!"

I'm so surprised by the outburst that I don't know what to say.
Not that there'd be any point in arguing with M. Desobry. He is
obviously panic-stricken—terrified of reprisals—and why not? Just
two days ago two British airplanes were shot down near here, and
despite heavy ground fire, five crewmen from the planes were able
to parachute to safety. Everyone assumes they've been hidden by
the underground—including the Germans, who have plastered posters everywhere warning that anyone caught hiding enemy pilots
or agents will immediately be arrested and shot. The Germans have
also taken sixteen prominent citizens as hostages, threatening to shoot
two of them each day until whoever is hiding the pilots gives them
up.

With a wife and eight children to worry about, it's no wonder
Desobry doesn't want me coming around anymore.

July 27, 1942. Back in Toulouse. As usual, I head straight to the
Banque de Bruxelles, where, mixing in with the other customers, I
can get a good look at M. Cartigny in his teller's cage. When I'm
confident that the coast is clear, I walk by him a couple of times
until I'm sure he's spotted me. After a few minutes, Cartigny gives
me the signal to come up to his window.

Cartigny has a note for me from Sabot, summoning me to Le
Petit Escargot for what turns out to be our last meeting together.
It seems my description has appeared in the Gestapo's black book,

which the Nazis publish monthly and distribute to local police to help them identify "criminals" wanted by the Reich. As a result, Sabot says, it's no longer safe for me to continue running the Pyrenees line. I'm to make just one more crossing—to show the route to the agent who has been picked to replace me, a young Belgian aristocrat code-named Leopold. After that, I'm to return to Brussels to await further instructions.

Almost casually, Sabot adds that I won't be working for him anymore. From now on, I'll be reporting directly to Charlotte.

I don't know what to say. I've learned so much from Sabot; I've come to rely on his judgment so completely. I can't imagine working for anyone else.

I remember how cold Sabot seemed to me after my first trip across the Pyrenees. I was so excited, telling him every detail of what was for me one of the most difficult and challenging accomplishments of my life so far. And all he had to say was, "Oh well, you'll get used to it. The more you cross, the easier it will become."

I couldn't believe how hard and inhuman he was. But the more I worked with him, the more I came to understand and appreciate his attitudes. I even began to imitate him in certain ways. For instance, whenever I recruit a new agent, I always make it very clear, just as we're shaking hands on it, that the recruit should think the whole thing over once more. And I remind him that an agent's long-term chances of survival are "almost nil." That's just what Sabot does. (Strangely enough, even though I know that that's correct, I am still convinced that I personally will survive the war. I keep making plans of what I'm going to do after the war. I can no more conceive of my not being around than I can conceive of the Allies not winning in the end.)

I mumble something to Sabot about how I'll miss him. He shakes my hand warmly and tells me I have the makings of a first-class agent. Then he returns to his work—as cold and businesslike as ever.

July 29, 1942. To a fleabag hotel on a small street just off the Boulevard Alsace-Lorraine to meet Leopold, the agent who is to take my place running the Pyrenees line. He turns out to be a nattily dressed young dandy—not at all my image of a mountain courier. Still, he's certainly eager enough. He pesters me with questions about my experience as a courier. When I tell him we won't be leaving for Osseja until Saturday, he practically collapses with disappointment.

Later I meet with Fabien, a former policeman who heads up the sector of my network that runs all the way from Toulouse to the Pyrenees, and with my main contact in Auch, a Belgian woman who has been living there ever since the war began and who has some useful contacts in the local government. I tell them both that I may be gone for some time, and I warn them about the Gestapo's increasing success in penetrating our lines. My instructions are simple: suspected double agents should be cut off from the network without hesitation. Quick and decisive action is essential in such cases, if we are to survive.

Finally, I go to see M. Cartigny. I tell him that it may be a while before he sees me again, and I share with him my doubts about Adolphe Manet.

August 1, 1942. A clear, sunny day—perfect weather for a crossing. At 9:00 A.M. I collect Leopold at his hotel. To my surprise, he's wearing a light suit and dressy shoes. Does he think we're going on a holiday outing? (As always, I have on my corduroy trousers, leather jacket, and heavy boots. Even in midsummer, it gets very cold in the mountains at night.)

On the way to the train station, I give Leopold a new identity card and remind him that he's not to sit or speak with me on the way to Osseja. He nods gravely, staring at me with such obvious admiration that it's almost embarrassing.

We arrive in Osseja in the middle of the afternoon. Leopold is ten meters behind me as I cross the Grand Place to the Hotel Calvet. With his slight build and dressy clothes, he looks like he might be a patient at one of the many sanatoriums in the area.

At the Calvet, Rene, the hotel keeper, gives us my regular room— number nine. Leopold is as excited as a schoolboy.

Early in the evening we're joined by Salvador, one of the leaders of the Spanish network. Salvador is only a few years older than me, a staunch idealist who fought on the Republican side during the

civil war here and practically worships the poet Unamuno. He takes
one look at Leopold and frowns. "Surely he doesn't expect to cross
the mountains dressed like that," he says to me in Spanish.

"What can we do?" I reply. "It's all he has."

Salvador shakes his head unhappily and explains that we may have
a problem getting over to Spain. It seems he hasn't been able to
find us a guide willing to go all the way to Ribas. "The best I can
do is get you a man who'll take you as far as the border," he says.
"After that, you'll be on your own."

I glance over at Leopold, who's been listening to our conversation.
He's only just started learning Spanish, and I'm not sure how much
he's understood.

"You ready for a little adventure?" I ask him.

He nods so eagerly that I can't help but smile. He'll learn soon
enough.

We leave the hotel with our guide around 8:30 in the evening. There's
no moon, but the sky is filled with stars. Leopold has a headache.
It's probably the altitude—that and a touch of nerves.

As usual, we begin by climbing through the forest. Leopold does
his best to keep up, but his fancy shoes keep slipping on the grass,
and he falls down several times. By the time we reach the goat
paths above the forest, he's drenched with sweat and shivering with
cold. His shoes look like they're about to fall apart.

We reach the top of the pass around 1:00 A.M. Leopold is so
excited to have reached the highest point of the crossing that, for a
moment at least, he seems to forget his exhaustion. I don't think
he realizes that in some ways the climb down is a lot more difficult
than the climb up.

While Leopold tries to figure out exactly where the border is—
like a schoolboy, he wants to stand with one foot planted in France,
the other in Spain—the guide helps me locate some landmarks up
ahead. Then he turns back to Osseja, leaving Leopold and me to
start our descent into Spain.

Moving slowly and carefully in the darkness, we begin to make
our way down the rocky incline. Before long, the sole of one of
Leopold's shoes comes loose. He wraps a handkerchief around it,
but it doesn't do very much good. Soon his foot is bleeding.

We press on. Just as the sky begins to lighten, we catch sight of Ribas far below us. By now, both of Leopold's shoes have fallen apart, and he is walking in his heavy, woolen socks. He doesn't say anything, but it's clear he's in a lot of pain. "Just two more hours," I tell him. He winces. In his condition, two hours probably seems like an eternity.

August 2, 1942. We reach the safe house around eleven in the morning—several hours behind schedule. The concierge gives us something to drink, then ushers us upstairs to the bedroom for some badly needed sleep.

I wake up around 2:00 P.M. Leopold is dead to the world. I decide to leave him be.

Ramon arrives from Barcelona an hour or so later. We exchange envelopes, and then I go upstairs to rouse Leopold. He doesn't want to get out of bed, but I don't give him any choice. We'll be starting back in a few hours, and he must get some food into him before we go.

Over dinner, Ramon and I try to teach Leopold to drink wine the way the Spanish do—*a la regalade*—pouring it down your throat without letting the bottle touch your lips. He's game, but clumsy.

We leave the house at six. Though tired, Leopold is in good spirits—mainly because we've found him a pair of espadrilles to replace his ruined shoes.

By seven we're above the tree line. The sun is going down, and a light mist covers the horizon. I show Leopold a trick that enables you to see the crest even when it's foggy: you lay down on the ground and sight up the slope, in effect looking under the fog. He tries it several times but can't seem to get the knack.

As we climb, the mist thickens. Soon we're completely socked in—can't see a thing. Leopold starts to get nervous, asking me if we're lost. We are, but I don't want to tell him yet. We keep climbing blindly. Around midnight it starts to rain. With no moon or stars to navigate by, with no landmarks visible, I have no idea where we are. All we can do is keep climbing.

Around 2:00 A.M. I find a small cave where we can rest. It's too cold and wet to sleep, but too dark and slippery to try to continue on. We huddle in the cave, moving our legs constantly to keep from freezing.

August 3, 1942. Around 5:00 A.M. the sky begins to lighten, and we push on. It turns out we're just a few meters from one of the small cement posts that mark the exact line of the frontier. Leopold is so relieved that he laughs aloud.

The temperature rises quickly as the sun climbs higher in the sky, and we have no trouble following the Ariege River down toward Osseja. Leopold is in high spirits, gazing at the scenery, admiring the crystalline clarity of the cowbells that tinkle in the distance. He even begins to sing.

I'm not so lighthearted. We're way behind schedule. Not only will Salvador be worried about us, but also the later we arrive, the more likely we'll be to run into border guards.

Fortunately, none seem to be about. We stroll into Osseja unmolested, just as the church bell tolls noon.

Salvador is waiting for us at the hotel. He greets me with typical Spanish enthusiasm. "How dare you come here in the middle of the day?" he says, shaking his head.

I turn to Leopold. "You make the excuses," I tell him. "I'm going to bed."

August 6, 1942. How oppressive Brussels can be in the August heat. I'm staying with Commandant Castiaux, anxiously awaiting word from Charlotte about my new assignment. In the afternoon a meeting with Aristide and Marc. They tell me Charlotte is in London, and no one knows when (or if) he'll be back.

Aristide and Marc are every bit as frustrated as I am. Communications with London have just about broken down. Their complaints about shortages of money and equipment seem to have fallen on deaf ears. Instead of help, they've gotten nothing but contradictory advice and bizarre requests. Just the other week, they tell me, a message came through from the boys in London asking us to start sending them complete editions of Belgian newspapers. It's ridiculous—with the Gestapo cracking down, we can barely manage to smuggle out microfilm.

To make matters worse, the agents the British have been parachuting into the occupied territories are so ill prepared for the Gestapo's ruthless efficiency that most of them are arrested within hours of their arrival.

What can be going on over there? Many of our people are beginning to wonder if any of their material is getting through to London—and if it is, whether anyone in British intelligence bothers to read it. Morale is at an all-time low.

We decide to send a long, angry message to headquarters detailing just how bad things have gotten. Perhaps that will get their attention.

August 8, 1942. Word from London! Charlotte is to be dropped by parachute into France tomorrow, and I'm to meet him in Grenoble. Aristide thinks there's some sort of power struggle going on among the British intelligence chiefs. That could account for the conflicting signals we've been receiving. Whatever the case, I don't intend to mince any words when I see Charlotte. Things must improve.

August 9, 1942. In the morning Aristide drops off two large suitcases, crammed with microfilm and other documents, that I'm to bring with me to Grenoble. It's insanely dangerous to carry so much espionage material through the occupied territories—but so many of our agents have been arrested, and so many of our letter boxes have been raided, that I have no choice.

Aristide also gives me a gun. I don't like that at all. I'm an intelligence agent, not a saboteur. But Aristide is adamant, and I'm in too much of a hurry to argue. Instead, I stash the gun in one of the suitcases.

I take the train to Paris, then board a crowded bus to Chalon-sur-Saone, where I plan to stay the night with my agent there, the engineer Orset. Just outside Chalon, the bus is stopped by a roadblock. Two German Feldgendarmen get on, one entering through the front door, the other through the back. The Feldgendarmen are feared by everyone, even their own soldiers. As usual, I'm standing by the rear exit (I always take that spot in case I have to jump off quickly). As a result, the German who got on the back of the bus asks to see my papers first. Quite calmly, I hand him one of my phony identity cards.

As he studies my card, it hits me. I've given him the wrong one—

not my Paris card, but one from Bordeaux, all the way on the other side of France. The Feldgendarm frowns suspiciously and orders me and my suitcases off the bus.

Slowly, I climb down onto the road. While I wait there with the stolid-faced German, the other soldier checks everyone else's papers. Finally, he gets off the bus. As he approaches us, he asks his colleague in German who I am and what I'm doing in Chalon. This is my chance. Using my very best German, I immediately launch into an elaborate explanation, telling them I'm here on official business to see Orset. After all, Orset is well-known in the area for doing business with engineers from all over France. It's one of the things that makes him so valuable to the underground.

I suppose my German is better than that of most Frenchmen. Still, I can't get over how quickly the Feldgendarmen apparently decide I'm okay. Without even bothering to ask what's in my suitcases, they wish me a friendly "auf Wiedersehen" and tell me I can go. Struggling with the unwieldy suitcases, I make my way to Orset's house, going a little out of the way to make sure I'm not being tailed.

Orset gets very nervous when I tell him what's happened. Just because my German is good is no reason for the Feldgendarmen to be so nice to me, he says—unless they know that he works for the underground and are planning a raid. We sit there for a moment, wondering if we should try to flee. Then, suddenly, his wife begins to laugh.

Orset and I stare at her as if she's lost her mind.

She shakes her head, trying to calm down. "It just came to me," she says finally. "Raymond, you told the Feldgendarmen you were here to see Orset, didn't you?"

I nod, baffled.

"Well, that's it. They probably misunderstood you. I'll bet they thought you said you were here to see Orcel—not Orset."

Orset and I look at each other. Of course. Orcel is the pro-Nazi mayor of Chalon. The soldiers obviously assumed I was a fellow collaborator come to visit him.

August 10, 1942. By train to Grenoble, the picturesque ski resort at the foot of the French Alps. Our safe house here is a three-room flat on the third floor of a house owned by a wealthy man who's rarely around. In all, there are seven of us jammed into the small apartment—Charlotte and me, two radio operators (Charlotte calls them "pianists"), and three other couriers. They are all much older than me, vastly experienced and filled with stories of danger and daring.

August 13, 1942. I find it amazing how much Charlotte and his people can accomplish under such impossible circumstances. They work all night, sweating and swearing in the cramped apartment, coding and decoding messages with their cipher grids. Then each morning at seven, the pianists load their suitcase radios into a deserted cable car and ride to the top of the mountain, where they make contact with London.

Today I accompany them, acting as a lookout. The mountains are beautiful in the morning, covered with a fresh blanket of snow that makes the world seem innocent and peaceful.

August 14, 1942. At last, my meeting with Charlotte. All my complaints about London's stupidity and incompetence come spilling out. To my surprise, Charlotte agrees with most of them. Things can't go on like this, he says, and they won't. As Aristide guessed, there's been some sort of power struggle going on over there—I'm unable to follow Charlotte's explanation of exactly who's involved and which side everyone is on—but it's over now and things are bound to get better.

That settled, Charlotte gives me my new assignment. I'm to check the security of all the courier lines serving all our networks from Belgium to Spain. We've been badly penetrated by the Gestapo, and my job will be to discover just where the weak links are. To this end, Charlotte gives me a supply of sealing wax and a small coin, with which I am to seal a series of test packages that will be sent along suspect lines. By checking the seals at various letter boxes, we should be able to find out exactly where our traffic is being tampered with—and on that basis, isolate rotten sections of the network.

Charlotte also shows me a copy of the Gestapo's black book so I can see for myself just how much the Germans know about me. It's

unnerving. They describe me so accurately that I'm amazed I've
survived this long.

August 15, 1942. By train to Toulouse, to begin testing the security
of our lines. I'm greeted with tragic news. While I was away, a
section chief of mine began to suspect that one of his two brothers
was a double agent. He worried about the problem for several days,
then—convinced that the brother posed a threat to the entire network,
and mindful of my instructions to act decisively—ordered another
agent to kill him. Somehow, his orders were garbled, and the wrong
brother was killed.

August 18, 1942. I celebrate my twenty-first birthday by discovering
what I think is a weak link in the courier section operating out of
Auch. It looks as if one of our agents has been passing information to the Vichy police. Nothing to do but close down his letter
box. (Some of the men want the traitor killed, but after last week's
mix-up, I refuse to sanction any executions.)

August 25, 1942. I've identified another rotten leg of our line. The
wax on a series of packages that I personally sealed and sent from
Roubaix to Paris has clearly been tampered with. There's no time
to find out which of our agents is the traitor—the whole section
will have to be cut off. That means closing down two letter boxes
and losing three or four couriers along with twelve to fifteen information sources. It's a painful loss, but what choice do I have?

August 30, 1942. My report to Charlotte is a gloomy one. Gestapo
reprisals against civilians suspected of helping the underground are
growing increasingly vicious. As a result, many former sympathizers
have begun closing their doors to our people. To make matters worse,
the Germans have drastically stepped up the number of security
checks and border patrols, making life more dangerous for every
agent—especially the couriers, who must travel from region to region
and country to country.

If Charlotte is surprised by any of this, he doesn't show it. He
has a more pressing problem on his mind—the situation in Holland.

The Dutch underground, he tells me, is in a shambles. Worse than a shambles, in fact. According to London, it's been completely penetrated by the Gestapo—to the point where hardly a network in the country is secure. Not only are the Germans aware of everything the Dutch resistance is up to, in some cases they may actually be calling the shots—controlling the activities of entire networks through well-placed double agents.

In part, Charlotte says, this disaster may be the fault of SOE— the Special Operations Executive established by the British two years ago to coordinate and direct all resistance activities in occupied Europe. Charlotte suspects that SOE has consistently underestimated the enemy's counterespionage abilities in Holland—in some cases failing to take the most elementary precautions to protect the underground groups it's been supporting.

For the first time, I'm beginning to get a sense of just whom I'm really working for. SOE must be the mysterious "boys in London" who've been sending us all those ridiculous orders. I must say, they really are hard to figure out. Not long ago, for example, they asked us to start sending them the latest issues of dozens of local newspapers and magazines. It's difficult enough smuggling out microfilmed intelligence data. Don't they realize that heavy, bulky stacks of newspapers are bound to be noticed by the Feldpolizei and the Gestapo?

In any case, Queen Wilhelmina of the Netherlands has secretly asked the Belgian government-in-exile to help her establish a new underground organization in Holland. The matter, Charlotte adds, is so sensitive—so fraught with both political and security implications—that, for now at least, neither the Dutch intelligence service nor the SOE are to know about it.

I look at Charlotte, puzzled. If all this is so secret—and I can well understand why it should be—why is he telling me about it?

Charlotte returns my gaze silently. He knows what I'm thinking, but he wants me to figure it out for myself.

I stare at the floor, my mind racing. Of course. The answer is obvious. They want me to organize this new Dutch underground. "But surely there are people more experienced," I protest, "people better suited than me."

Charlotte shakes his head and begins ticking off points with his fingers. "One, you've shown yourself to be an innovative leader with strong organizational skills. Two, you're a quick study. Three, you speak fluent Dutch." He smiles at me. "Shall I go on?"

I suppose it makes sense. Still, I can't believe it. Me, a twenty-one-year-old Belgian, in charge of the Dutch resistance. What a strange war—what a strange world—this is.

Having been given carte blanche in organizing the new Dutch network—another way of saying he was completely on his own—Gaston returned to Brussels to confer with Aristide and Marc about borrowing some of their people. He had decided to cover southeastern Holland with Belgian agents operating out of Ghent and Antwerp. Dutch agents would be recruited and used for the southwest and north.

Chapter Seven

WIM

September 8, 1942. Back in Brussels, staying as usual with the Castiaux family. The commandant's daughter, Violette, is hoping I'll be able to come to a reunion of the 533d that she's organized for next Sunday. I'd love to, but there's no way I can. Not without asking for trouble from the Gestapo.

I've been thinking about a name for my new organization and have decided on "WIM," after Queen Wilhelmina. (I like the fact that it reads the same upside down—should save me time when I'm stamping documents.)

I also need a new cover name for myself—a Dutch name. After considering a host of alternatives, I settle on Rinus. No particular reason. I guess I just like the sound of it.

September 9, 1942. My first recruit for WIM. His name is John Cohen, and he's a Dutch Jew who has been living in Spain, where he fought against the Fascists during the civil war. Actually, I didn't really recruit John. Charlotte sent him to me (which means I don't have to worry about his bona fides). I shall put him in charge of southeastern Holland.

I find it hard to sleep tonight. Tomorrow I'll be returning to Ghent (to recruit agents) for the first time since I left home sixteen months ago. I'd give anything to be able to see my parents and sister. If only I could visit them without jeopardizing both their safety and mine.

September 10, 1942. Disguised in a gray slouch hat and thick eyeglasses, I take the late-evening train to Ghent. As usual, it's crowded with commuters coming home after a day's work in the capital. As we pull into Sint Pieter Station, I'm overwhelmed with a wave of homesickness. I could be home, sitting at the kitchen table with my parents, in just a few minutes. And a few minutes after that, no doubt, the Gestapo would be knocking at the door.

Instead, I go to see my cousins, Georgette and Laurent Delfosse. They live in Mariakerke, on the other side of Ghent from my parents. It's a long way to walk from the train station, but I don't mind—it gives me time to think. (It's also easier to avoid tails on foot.) Georgette and Laurent are delighted to see me, and we wind up talking late into the night, exchanging news. My parents, thank goodness, are fine. They've even been enjoying fresh eggs and potatoes— courtesy of my cousin, Laurent, who live near farmers.

September 11, 1942. In the morning, I have Georgette deliver a message to my old school friend Max. Though Max has finally realized his boyhood dream and become a policeman, he's still a patriot. I'm counting on him to help me recruit agents for WIM.

September 12, 1942. To a café in Sint Martens-Lathem to meet with Max. What a treat to see him again after all this time. He's put on some weight and looks a lot older—but other than that he doesn't seem to have changed very much.

As I'd hoped, Max is eager to help me get WIM organized and running. There's a lot he can do. As a policeman, Max is in an ideal position to check the reliability of potential agents. He also knows plenty of people as eager as he is to work for the resistance.

September 14, 1942. To Antwerp for the day to contact some people suggested by Max. One of them is a woman named Rosa whose husband owns a butcher shop that would make a perfect letter box.

Another is a nurse who's been hiding Jews and Allied pilots who've been shot down. Both women agree to start recruiting agents for me.

Setting up a network, I have discovered, is rather like growing a crystal in chemistry class. You prepare your supersaturated solution (in this case, the vast number of ordinary people who want to do something to fight the Germans), then drop in the seed (me), and let the laws of nature do the rest. As a result, I probably won't have to recruit too many more agents myself. The people I've recruited so far—and the people they recruit—will keep the chain growing. At least I hope that's the way it works out. The fewer people in the organization who know me personally, the better off we'll all be.

September 15, 1942. Staying with Commandant Castiaux again. I worry about endangering him and his family, but he seems to regard it as a matter of pride not to be intimidated by the German threats of reprisal.

Castiaux tells me of a neighbor of his, a Dutch broker with relatives in Holland, whom he believes would make an excellent agent for WIM. We invite the man over, and he turns out to be enthusiastic about helping the underground. As his work takes him to Holland regularly, he is in a perfect position to recruit people and set up letter boxes for us.

September 30, 1942. WIM is beginning to gather momentum—adding dozens of agents each week. We owe a lot to Marc and Aristide. Their radio operators have been serving as my pipeline to the BBC in London. As WIM is a new organization, my ability to get the BBC to broadcast special messages verifying its bona fides is absolutely crucial. I've been sending requests to London almost daily asking for a radio operator of my own, but so far I've had no reply.

October 1, 1942. After a day and a night in Antwerp, I'm up early to catch the train to Brussels. I've got to leave for the station before the curfew ends—at an hour during which only workers with special passes are allowed on the streets. As a result, Max—who's here on a detective assignment he wangled—agrees to accompany me.

As we cross a bridge near the station, we spot a German security patrol at the other end, checking identity cards. My instinct is to

turn and run, but we're too close to do that without attracting attention. I hesitate, but Max reacts instantly, shoving his gun and badge
into my hands and telling me to use them to get through the security
check. "Don't worry about me," he says. "I can talk my way out of
any trouble."

I hope he's right. I walk on ahead, flash Max's badge at the Germans,
and continue on my way without looking back.

No problem getting to Brussels. I'm staying in the Rue Americaine,
in the room above Jean Van Cauwenberghe's garage. I've been spending a lot of time holed up in such rooms lately, wading through the
flood of material that has come pouring in from my new WIM agents.
A lot of the people we've recruited have been gathering intelligence
on their own since the beginning of the war. Now that they've finally
got someone to give it to, there's no stopping them—it's like a dam
has burst.

Unfortunately, not all the material is worth sending. It takes me
hours and hours to go through it all, coding what little good stuff
there is for shipment to Spain.

October 15, 1942. WIM is growing by leaps and bounds, with already
more than two hundred agents throughout Holland. Yet I still can't
get London to send us a single radio operator. What is going on
over there?

I'm also having trouble getting my special messages broadcast over
the BBC. It's bad enough having to channel everything through
radio operators in Belgium and France, but lately it's become apparent
that the older Dutch networks—some of which we know have been
penetrated by the Gestapo—are getting much quicker and more
efficient responses to their requests than we are. I simply can't understand it.

October 23, 1942. So much raw intelligence is pouring into Rosa's
letter box that I've given up trying to code it all. There simply isn't
enough time. It's shocking how much of the material is devoted to
detailed accounts of political squabbling between various Dutch political factions. You'd think these people could rally around one simple
ideal: the need to defeat the Germans. Instead, they seem more

concerned with which group is going to have what power after the war is over, and who should go to London to inform the "authorities" about so-and-so's "unreliable political tendencies."

October 27, 1942. Been getting reports that a Dutch operative known as Piet Van de Velde, whose messages I'm constantly hearing on the BBC and Radio Oranje, may not be entirely trustworthy. There isn't any hard evidence against him. Still, I find it hard to accept that someone who is even slightly questionable should be able to get special messages through faster and easier than me.

November 1, 1942. Still no radio operator from London. Not even a response to my requests. What is the Dutch government-in-exile doing? You'd think they'd give me the support I need. After all, they're the ones who asked me to do all this for them.

November 6, 1942. I'm beginning to wonder if these Dutch hate each other more than they hate the Germans. Their main interest seems to be in who will run things after the war. Don't they realize we have to win the war first?

I've given up trying to get London to send me a radio operator. At this point I'm willing to settle for just a radio with instructions on how to use it.

What Gaston didn't know—indeed, couldn't know—was that he was caught up in one of the most ingenious and perplexing counterintelligence coups of the war: the German operation known as Das Englandspiel. *Early the previous March, counterintelligence officers from the Gestapo and Abwehr had arrested a British agent named Hubert Lauwers in The Hague. Lauwers had been parachuted into the Netherlands with a radio transmitter to establish direct communications between resistance leaders on the ground and SOE headquarters in London. After several days of intense Gestapo interrogation, Lauwers agreed to continue transmitting to London as if he hadn't been captured—though unbeknownst to his British masters, he would now be sending messages prepared by the Germans.*

In fact, Lauwers's decision to cooperate was quite sensible. Like all British agents, he had been provided with what was known as a "security check"—a code word or phrase that would normally be inserted into every message he transmitted as a sign that all was well. Omitting the security check or sending it incorrectly would signal London that an agent was operating under duress of some sort. Lauwers was thus confident that with his very first phony message his superiors would realize his predicament and at the very least figure out some way of turning the situation to their advantage.

To his dismay, they did not. Although Lauwers garbled or scrambled his security check in every message he sent under German control, London continued to regard his transmissions as secure. Even when Lauwers risked his life by including the English word "caught" in the Dutch text of several of his messages, headquarters remained oblivious. For the next twelve months, the chiefs of the SOE's Dutch section blindly accepted the cleverly fabricated Gestapo and Abwehr signals that Lauwers transmitted as genuine messages from resistance leaders. What's more, SOE transmitted back to Lauwers and his captors an intelligence windfall for the Germans: the arrival times and precise locations where new agents and materiel would be dropped into the Netherlands as well as details of Allied strategy.

As a result, the Germans were able not only to monitor but actually to direct all of SOE's Dutch operations. Eventually, the Germans came to infiltrate and control the entire Dutch underground. Using Lauwers and other captured radio operators, they arranged for nearly two hundred parachute drops of British agents and materiel—all of which fell right into the waiting arms of the Gestapo. Over the next eighteen months, some fifty-eight Anglo-Dutch agents were captured—most within moments of touching down on Dutch soil. All but four of them were executed.

More than forty years later, the question of why London disregarded Lauwers's warning signals remains unanswered. One possible explanation—the simplest one—was that there were German agents at work right in the heart of SOE headquarters. Another was that London knew what was happening but for the sake of some larger strategy—Le Grand Jeu, as it became known—chose to ignore it. Unfortunately, the secret records that might have contained the answer were destroyed in a mysterious fire that swept through SOE's offices shortly after the end of the war.

November 9, 1942. One of my agents reports that Piet Van de Velde's real name is Vanderwaals, and that he's actually a double agent in the pay of the Germans. Yet London continues to transmit his messages, while mine are blocked. Could it be that the Dutch in London don't trust me because I'm Belgian?

November 15, 1942. The Gestapo has begun spreading rumors that Rinus is a double agent working for them. A tribute, I suppose, to WIM's growing effectiveness.

I'm back in Brussels to confer with Aristide about recruiting some more Belgian agents for WIM—in particular, trustworthy survivors of La Brigade Blanche and the Luctor et Emergo network, both of which were smashed by the Gestapo last summer. I don't know what I'd do without my Belgian contacts. Everything touched by Holland seems to be poisoned.

November 19, 1942. Still no radios from London. A contact of mine in Hilversum knows some electrical engineers who may be able to build us some sets from scratch. I'm beginning to think London is deliberately ignoring us. Could there be double agents over there?

December 1, 1942. Word from Rosa that our cross-border line to Belgium may have been penetrated. Supposedly, there is a traitor among our agents at Hilversum. I must see what I can find out.

December 2, 1942. I meet with my agent Stenger, just back from The Hague, and ask him to go to Hilversum to investigate Rosa's report. If he has any doubts about any of our agents, we will abandon the line immediately.

I'm currently in Putte, staying with people I don't know—friends of Stenger's brother-in-law. Stenger insists they're okay, but I don't like it. Strangers make me nervous.

December 4, 1942. Stenger is back with unsettling word. One of Oom Henk's agents told him he'd been contacted by a Dutchman who said he was in direct contact with London. Even claimed he could get special messages broadcast on the BBC—on just one day's notice. What *is* going on?

December 12, 1942. Worrisome news from Georgette and Laurent Delfosse. The Gestapo has been back to see my family, demanding information about me—namely, where I am and when the last time was that they saw me. Though Georgette has told my parents that she's heard I'm fine, she's never let on that I've been staying with her and Laurent in Ghent—or that she's even seen me. As far as my parents know, I could be in England.

December 25, 1942. I'm in Tourcoing with my old friends the Dujardins for *three whole days* of badly needed rest. A lovely Christmas present this morning from Margot. She managed to get hold of one of my favorite opera records and surprised me by playing it when I woke up. I had to bury my face in the newspaper. Didn't want her to see me crying.

In the evening she and Robert go off to a party. It's quite late when they return. Robert is very drunk, shouting at the top of his lungs about what he'd like to do to "those pigs, the Boches." When Margot tries to quiet him down, he turns on her, and soon they are arguing bitterly about all sorts of personal things. It's horrible—such a contrast to this morning.

January 10, 1943. Commandant Castiaux says there's been some trouble at his office downtown—a couple of his close friends were arrested and put into the prison at St. Gilles. I'm worried that if I don't stop staying with him, he may be next.

The WIM organization continues to spread like wildfire. We're now active in every province and major city in Holland. In all, we've currently got more than twelve hundred agents—only a handful of whom have ever seen my face or know that I'm not Dutch. (I wonder what they'd say if someone told them their chief was a Belgian—a twenty-one-year-old Belgian at that.)

I'm proud of my anonymity—though it may be at least partly responsible for the persistence of the Gestapo-spread rumors that Rinus is a double agent. The real problem, of course, is our continuing inability to get WIM's special messages relayed by the BBC as quickly as some other so-called resistance groups here—groups that I know are riddled with traitors. I've got to get London to acknowledge publicly that I'm their bona fide representative in Holland.

January 15, 1943. No response yet to my request that the BBC broadcast a message stating once and for all that Rinus is not a double agent. What's maddening is that I've heard that a number of operatives over here (among them, the Dutch military attaché in Switzerland) have received queries from London asking them to check me out. Don't they know who I am?

It's ridiculous. WIM is currently sending London nearly a thousand microfilmed pages of military, economic, and political intelligence each week. That includes hundreds of maps detailing the location of German antiaircraft installations, Wehrmacht barracks, Gestapo headquarters, railroad tracks regularly used by cement trains, and so on. Also a copy of each issue of every underground newspaper and long lists of Dutch officials who are collaborating with the Nazis—as well as those who pretend to collaborate but actually help us, secretly providing WIM agents with identity cards, ration coupons, and the like.

As if all that weren't enough, through our system of coast watchers we manage to keep London informed of the exact location and size of all German bunkers and heavy artillery. What more could they want!

January 19, 1943. This morning the BBC finally began broadcasting the special message I'd been begging them to send: "Rinus is the good father of Jan, WIM, and John." If that doesn't put an end to the double-agent rumors, I don't know what will. About bloody time, as the British would say.

January 25, 1943. Staying at Jean Van Cauwenberghe's garage, working on a plan to get the exact layout of Gestapo headquarters here in Brussels. Gaston Garreyn has been delivering milk there, and in the process he's developed some inside connections who may be able to furnish him with a floor plan of the place. It seems that when the Gestapo took over the place—formerly a grand private home—they kicked out the owners but allowed the couple who served them as maid and butler to stay. What the Germans don't know is that the couple is pro-British. With their help, Garreyn is slowly putting together a map of the place.

January 26, 1943. Worrisome message from John Cohen. One of our section chiefs in Holland has been contacted by a group of "Dutch patriots" who want WIM to help them evacuate three British pilots who were supposedly shot down last week. I don't like it. We're an intelligence network, not an evacuation line. Anyway, there haven't been any reports of any British pilots bailing out over Holland in the last few days.

I send back word ordering our section chief not to cooperate. Too much of a risk that those so-called British pilots are really German counterintelligence agents in disguise.

February 3, 1943. More rumors that WIM lines have been penetrated by German agents. Each time we isolate a traitor, another one seems to burrow in somewhere else.

What is it that makes people turn against their neighbors and side with the enemy? Fear? Greed? I simply can't understand it.

February 12, 1943. The Gestapo has been back to see my parents. Georgette tells me not to worry: If worst comes to worst, she says, my mother and father can hide with her and Laurent.

February 15, 1943. After conferring with Aristide and Marc, I send word to London that the Germans seem to be closing in on me, and that it's time I finally left the Continent. The fact is, I want to go to London to see for myself just what's going on over there.

February 17, 1943. Word from Grenoble that Charlotte wants to see me. Perhaps headquarters has responded to my request to go to London.

February 18, 1943. Uneventful journey to Grenoble, if any journey across two enemy borders during wartime can be called uneventful. I arrive at the safe house to find our three-room apartment crowded with six other agents, one of them an attractive young woman in her early twenties. Her name is Violaine, and she has long blonde hair and an infectious smile.

As usual, everyone is hard at work coding and decoding messages. Nonetheless, the atmosphere in the cramped apartment is lighthearted, almost gay, with people exchanging jokes and reminiscences as they work. It's like a party, really, and as the night wears on, the conversation becomes louder and more animated, the jokes dirtier and more filled with sexual innuendo.

At first I can't believe the men are carrying on like this in front of a girl. But Violaine turns out to be just as uninhibited as the men. Indeed, if anything, her vocabulary is a lot more profane. At one point she describes in graphic terms a new way of making love that she's discovered: in a bathtub filled with three inches of warm water.

Violaine fascinates me, and not just because she's so pretty. I've never met anyone like her before, at least not any girl. She's self-reliant, outspoken, the kind of person who enjoys throwing out provocative statements just to get a rise out of people. She clearly considers herself the equal of any man, and she's probably right.

One of the other agents tells me that Violaine comes from an aristocratic French family with a long history of diplomatic service. Her father's currently the Vichy ambassador to Switzerland. She joined the resistance in Paris right after the German invasion and since then has become a skilled (though sometimes reckless) agent, highly valued by the French underground.

It's well after midnight by the time all the coding has been completed. Momentarily, I wonder where in these close quarters Violaine is going to sleep. I have to laugh at my naivete. Obviously, she'll sleep anywhere she chooses.

February 19, 1943. In the morning to the top of the mountain with the pianists, to stand watch while they transmit the day's message traffic. When we finally return to the safe house late in the day, Charlotte tells me that he's still waiting for a decision on my request to go to London. In the meantime, he wants me to go to Perpignan to set up a new courier line into Spain, which we can use as a backup if our old Raymond-Ramon line is ever cut. I'm to leave on the night train with Violaine. We'll be traveling as brother and sister, sharing a single sleeping compartment.

Though the night train is crowded, a sleeper has been reserved for Violaine and me, and we have no trouble getting on. Our compartment is small but comfortable, with bunk beds and a tiny sink. Violaine chooses the lower berth, and I step into the corridor to give her some privacy while she changes into her nightclothes. When I come back in, she whispers for me to climb in beside her so we can talk.

It's the first time I've ever shared a bed with an attractive young woman in a negligee. I certainly hope it's not the last.

Violaine tells me that Charlotte thinks I'm very special, different from the usual run of agent. He's evidently quite impressed that someone as young as me shows so much initiative. Also by the fact that I'm always reading, trying to keep up with my studies. It's strange to hear these things. Pleasant, but also a bit puzzling. Am I really that special?

Later we talk about the future. Violaine wants to know what I plan to do after the war. I tell her of my love for physics and mathematics, how I hope to get my doctorate one day and do research at a university. She says she wants to be a diplomat like her father. (I find that funny—this uninhibited, unconventional girl talking about becoming a diplomat.)

We talk on and on. At dawn the train begins to slow; then, abruptly and unexpectedly, it screeches to a halt. We sit up in alarm. We're not supposed to arrive in Perpignan for another two hours. Worried, we peer out the window. A platoon of German soldiers is lined up along the side of the track. As we watch, they begin to board the train, several cars ahead of us.

Violaine immediately starts pulling on her clothes, getting ready to make a break for it. I shake my head and tell her to get back in bed. The train is surrounded. There's nothing we can do but sit tight and stick to our cover story: we're brother and sister on our way to visit relatives in Perpignan.

The minutes drag on. We can hear the wail of frightened women and children echoing down the corridor as the soldiers search the train. It's only a matter of time before they knock on our door.

Suddenly, we hear a huge hiss of steam, and the train lurches into motion. Violaine and I look around in surprise. A Gestapo trick? I peer out the window. The German patrol is marching off, dragging with them a miserable-looking Frenchman, his hands tied behind his back. That's the way war is. One man's misfortune is another's good luck.

February 20, 1943. The train pulls into Perpignan around 9:00 A.M. Violaine and I leave the station together, then a quick embrace and we go our separate ways. Will I ever see her again? I doubt it.

I make my way to an old building on the Rue de la Lanterne, where an agent of mine—a journalist named Lucrece—runs a safe house and letter box out of a third-floor apartment. According to Lucrece, the Gestapo has put a price on Raymond's head. How flattering. If they only knew that Raymond has turned into Rinus.

Gaston remained in Perpignan for three weeks, setting up the new backup courier route to Spain. It turned out to be time well spent. As Charlotte had feared, the old Raymond-Ramon line had just about reached the end of its useful life. Leopold, the eager young aristocrat who had replaced Gaston on the Osseja-Ribas run, was caught and arrested after making only one trip.

Once he got the new line up and running, Gaston spent the next month or so roaming around the Continent checking the security of WIM's other courier lines and monitoring the organization's operations. In fact, he was killing time, waiting to hear from London.

While he waited, WIM continued to grow, adding as many as a dozen new people in a single day. Often, WIM recruiters would stumble across a ready-made cell of would-be agents already at work in some government office or other. These were usually patriots who had belonged to one of the older resistance networks that had been smashed by the Nazis. Cut off from London, they had continued to gather information—sometimes for years—in the hope that they would eventually find a new pipeline to the Allies.

April 23, 1943. Still no word on my request to go to London. Both Aristide and Castiaux (with whom I'm staying) counsel patience. Aside from Charlotte, they're the only ones who know of my intention to go. When I think about it, I sometimes can't believe how much I'm able to keep secret. Just a handful of WIM agents (John, Stenger, Rosa, and a few others) even know what their chief looks like. And no one ever knows my travel plans in advance—including me.

April 26, 1943. Word has arrived from Grenoble. Charlotte wants to see me. Can this be it? Am I finally to be on my way to London?

May 3, 1943. The safe house in Grenoble is quiet and peaceful. Charlotte greets me with a big smile. It's just as I'd hoped. I'm to leave for London (by way of Spain) in a few days. If all goes well, I could be in England in a couple of weeks.

My passage to England, Charlotte tells me, should be straight-forward, if not simple. First I'm to go to Perpignan to check on some microfilm shipments. Then, across the Pyrenees to Barcelona, using one of the new lines I set up in March. From there, I'll continue on to Lisbon, where I'll be put on a boat or plane to London.

Tired out from my journey, I go to bed early—only to find I can't sleep. My mind is racing, wondering who and what I will meet in London. Charlotte won't tell me anything—for security reasons, he says. His caution makes me laugh. I'm certainly not about to let myself get captured now.

May 9, 1943. Back in Perpignan. How I love this old Moorish city, with its labyrinthine streets and tall, tropical palms. It seems especially attractive to me this sunny May morning—perhaps because I'm about to leave the Continent behind.

My first stop is my agent Lucrece's apartment on the Rue de la Lanterne. He's holding several hundred packs of butter—that is, microfilm—that I'm supposed to check. I've been using these shipments to test the security of our lines from Holland. With even more care than usual, I inspect the containers, then reseal them for shipment with the wax and coin Charlotte gave me. I'm not about to have anything go wrong on the eve of my departure.

After I finish sealing the containers, Lucrece gives me the key to his mother's apartment, where I'm to spend the night. I'll come back tomorrow to return the key, then make what I hope will be my last clandestine crossing of the Pyrenees. If all goes well, I'll be in London before I know it.

May 10, 1943. Another sunny morning. Three years to the day since the war came to Belgium. I try to remember what it was like back then, but I can't.

I make my way back to Lucrece's building, then climb the old staircase to the third floor and give his doorbell three quick turns. No one answers. Something is wrong.

I glance down the stairway. Suddenly, the door to Lucrece's apartment flies open. I turn to see two German Mausers pointed at me. A hand grabs the collar of my leather jacket and starts to pull me inside. I drop into a crouch and turn, slipping my arms out of the jacket sleeves. Then I bolt down the stairs—half running, half falling, scrambling desperately to keep my legs under me.

All around me more doors are opening. Suddenly, the staircase is flooded with German soldiers. I dive down the remaining flight, falling to my knees in the hallway leading to the front door. As I struggle to regain my feet, a rifle butt crashes into my back between my shoulders. The world disappears in an explosion of pain and I crumple to the floor.

Before I can recover, I'm grabbed by several sets of strong hands and dragged back up the stairs into one of the apartments. After a perfunctory search, I'm pitched into a closet filled with musty old clothes, and the door is locked behind me. I lie there in the dark for what seems like an eternity. "They've got you—they've finally got you," I keep thinking. I can't believe it. After all I've been through—to be captured now.

Every so often I hear shouts in German and the sounds of a struggle as the soldiers grab some other poor fool who has wandered into their trap. Since there aren't any microfilm drops scheduled for today, and no agent but me is supposed to be in the building, all the other victims are probably innocent residents or visitors who had no idea what was going on in Lucrece's apartment.

Though it's bad luck for them, it's a good sign for me. If the Germans are simply grabbing everyone who comes in, it means they probably don't know who I am.

I've got to make sure things stay that way. From the pile of old clothes in the closet, I select two coats. Carefully, I tear a small opening in each of their linings. In one of the linings, I hide my sealing wax; in the other, I slip Charlotte's coin—the only evidence to connect me with the microfilm containers I left in the apartment (which the Germans must have found by now). As far as the soldiers will know, I'm just one more innocent Frenchman who had the bad fortune to stumble into their net.

It's evening by the time they finally come for me. I've worked out a cover story to explain what I was doing in the building, but I don't get a chance to use it. Instead, I'm thrown into a truck with a number of other dazed and battered Frenchmen. We're driven to a large mansion that the Gestapo has taken over for use as its local headquarters.

The place echoes with the sound of screaming and beatings. As I'm brought upstairs, I hear an officer demanding that some poor wretch admit he is Raymond. So I'm right. They don't know who I am.

My arms handcuffed behind me, I'm led into a large room, where a short, slender officer in an impeccably tailored Gestapo uniform is sitting at a desk, flanked by a female secretary and two guards. In a sharp, high-pitched voice, the officer orders me to confess—he knows I'm the infamous Raymond, and the sooner I admit it, the better off I'll be.

Down the corridor, someone is alternately whimpering and screaming horribly. I didn't think human beings could make sounds like that. After one particularly bloodcurdling yell, the officer smiles and says that's one of my Spanish agents. "We're pulling out his fingernails one by one," he says.

I stare at the floor. The handcuffs they've put on me are the self-locking kind, which close tighter and tighter around your wrist each time you move, cutting off the circulation. The result is a horrible throbbing pain in my arms and shoulders. I take a deep breath. The man down the hall screams again.

"It's really up to you how much he suffers," the officer continues. "All you have to do is tell us what we want to know, and we'll be happy to stop."

He looks at me for a long moment. I say nothing.

"Then, again," the officer says, shaking his head, "perhaps when he runs out of fingernails, it will be necessary to start in on yours."

"You've got it all wrong," I protest. "I'm not who you think I am." The officer frowns and nods to the guards. First they lean on my handcuffs. The pain in my arms and back is excruciating. Then they hurl me against the wall and start punching me. Eventually, they knock me to the floor and begin taking turns kicking me with their heavy boots.

Part of me wishes I could tell them what I know. But there's no way I will. The one thing that both Sabot and Charlotte have drilled into me is the importance of not telling the Gestapo anything about anyone for at least forty-eight hours. Even at the risk of death, you've got to hold out, you've got to give your friends and colleagues time to learn of your arrest and take steps to protect themselves.

After a few minutes the soldiers stop their kicking and punching. The officer looks down at me and reads off a list of accusations— mainly acts of espionage—to which he wants me to confess. I tell him I have no idea who this Raymond is that he keeps talking about, and that in any case I'm too young to have done half of what he says I've done.

The officer shakes his head, and the guards resume beating me. The secretary, meanwhile, sits calmly in her chair at the side of the desk, sipping a cup of coffee, waiting for me to crack so she can start taking down my confession. Where do they find such people?

May 12, 1943. I've been in solitary confinement at Gestapo headquarters for the past two days. No food, hardly any water. Just a nearly continuous round of interrogation and beatings.

At one point, the guards grab me by the heels and swing me around in a circle, finally hurling me against a wall. Not certain I can take any more, I pretend to pass out. The guards poke at me halfheartedly, then one of them leaves the room. He returns a moment later with a snarling German shepherd. The dog strains at its leash trying to get at me. I continue to play dead. The guard eases off on the leash, and the dog goes for my throat. I can't help myself. Instinctively, I jerk my head back. The guards grin at each other, and the beating resumes.

May 13, 1943. This morning a break in the hellish routine. Instead of being taken once again to Gestapo headquarters for yet another interrogation session, I'm thrown into a truck and driven to the Perpignan prison—an old Moorish fortress that was once the palace of the kings of Majorca.

Unable to walk, I'm dragged down a corridor by two guards. Eventually, we arrive at an underground cell with a massive iron gate. The back of the cell opens onto a second, smaller cell, the front

wall of which is a grate of heavy steel bars. The guards fling me
into the tiny cell; lock the grate behind me; then go out through
the first cell, locking its iron door as they leave. I'm left alone in
the dark, sprawled on the filthy dirt floor. From what I can see
and smell, it seems that the last prisoner in here had been sick and
bleeding.

Left alone for the first time in three days, I finally get a chance
to examine myself. I'm covered with blood, and I think my jaw is
broken. The pain is excruciating. I still can't believe this is happening
to me—that I've actually been caught. That I might be killed.

May 14, 1943. After a painful and sleepless night, I'm taken from
my cell by two armed guards. They lead me at gunpoint into an
open yard, where they order me to drop my trousers and squat.
"Scheisse!" one of them shouts, waving his bayonet in my face. I
can't. All I can do is grimace in pain and fear.

Finally, I'm returned to my cell. At noon, the guards bring me a
tin bowl, which they fill with boiling soup. I'm desperate for nourishment, but the bowl is so hot that I can't hold it, and the soup spills
into the dirt. The guards find this very funny.

How can anyone believe there is a God? If he did exist, he wouldn't
let this happen. He would make it stop.

May 15, 1943. I'm brought back to Gestapo headquarters for more
questioning by the well-dressed officer. He continues to accuse me
of being Raymond, but it's clear he's no more certain of it than he
was the last time. I stick to my story: I'm just an innocent Frenchman
who's never heard of Raymond and knows nothing about any underground espionage.

After several hours of interrogation, I'm led into another room,
where a dark-haired young woman is being questioned. It's Braulia
Canovas, an agent of mine from Carcasson. The officer peers at us
closely, looking for any sign of recognition on either of our faces.
Neither of us gives anything away.

Then the guards start beating Braulia viciously. The officer tells
me all I have to do is identify her, and the beating will stop. I say
nothing. Angrily, he orders Braulia to identify me. She, too, remains
silent. After a while, I'm dragged out and beaten some more.

Later, as I lay in my cell, I find myself taunting God. Come on, I challenge him, prove yourself. Show me you exist. Do something to get me out of this.

But why should I expect any help from God (assuming he exists in the first place)? It wasn't God who put me here, it was *me*. I'm the one who chose to do what I did. I knew the risks. What was it I told every single person I recruited? "Unless you're ready and willing to give up your life for the cause, you shouldn't be doing this." Can't change the rules now.

May 20, 1943. Every day is the same. I'm dragged from my cell, questioned and beaten, then thrown back in. Both my nose and my jaw are broken, and one of my eyes is swollen shut. It's hard to eat, but I am determined not to break.

Lying in the dark, I keep picturing my father's face. He stares at me impassively, looking for signs of weakness, waiting for me to give up. I will surprise him. I will make him proud of me. I will not break.

Unknown to Gaston, not long after he was captured, his father was arrested by the Gestapo and sent to the concentration camp at Mauthausen. The Germans, of course, had no idea that in arresting Joseph Vandermeerssche they had arrested the father of the famous Raymond. Neither, for that matter, did Joseph. Indeed, it was only much later, after Gaston Garreyn was also captured and sent to Mauthausen, that Joseph found out that his son had been the head of WIM.

May 28, 1943. This morning after breakfast nearly fifty of us are put on trucks and driven to the train station, where we're packed so tightly into a third-class railway car that it's impossible to sit down. No one has any idea where they're taking us.

It turns out that half the prisoners on the train are named Raymond. Obviously, the Gestapo still doesn't know who I am.

Our train pulls into the Gare de l'Est in Paris late in the day. A large crowd watches sympathetically as we are let out of our car and marched down the platform. It would be so easy to dash into their midst and escape. But, no—the guards would probably fire into the crowd after me, and innocent people would surely die.

Once again we're loaded onto trucks. This time our destination is the Gestapo prison at Fresnes, a cheerless suburb just south of Paris. The prison is a forbidding place with a huge arched entryway flanked by two guardhouses. We're ordered off the trucks, led through the wrought-iron gate, then marched along a long wall of gray stone about ten meters high. Finally, we reach a heavy oak door. We're taken through one by one. A half dozen armed guards are waiting for us in a courtyard on the other side. Behind them are three long buildings, about five or six stories high, their featureless red-brick facades broken only by a series of tiny, barred windows.

My cell is a cramped, square room with a sink on one wall, a stout wooden door, and a postage-stamp-sized window just out of reach at the top of the far wall.

I must keep reminding myself: The longer I can keep them from finding out who I am, the safer my colleagues in France, Belgium, and Holland will be.

While Gaston languished in custody, the search for Raymond contin-ued throughout France. The Gestapo knew a lot about their quarry— that he controlled all of the courier lines and that he had personally created the Raymond-Ramon line through the Pyrenees. But they did not know that Raymond the courier and Rinus the chief of WIM were one and the same. Nor did they know that this enemy of the Reich had already fallen into their hands.

May 29, 1943. Just after breakfast I'm taken from my cell, bundled into a staff car, and driven back into Paris to the Gestapo headquarters on the Avenue Foch. Two guards lead me upstairs to a dingy room. After a few minutes an SD officer comes in. "You are Raymond?" he asks.

I stare at him blankly.

"Come on, young fellow," he says, frowning impatiently. "We know who you are."

"There's been a mistake," I reply. "I don't—"

Without warning, one of the guards smashes me in the face with his fist. I go flying against the wall.

"You are Raymond?" the officer repeats.

The process continues—the officer asking questions, me professing ignorance, the guards kicking and punching—for several hours.

June 1, 1943. I'm being kept in solitary, not allowed to see anyone but my guards and my inquisitors. Through the walls, however, I can hear another prisoner moving around in the cell next to mine. When the guards are busy elsewhere, I begin knocking on the wall in Morse code. "Qui est là?" I tap out. "Qui est là?"

Soon my neighbor begins to tap back. I strain to make out what he's sending, but it's confused, unclear. I repeat my message again. My neighbor responds with another burst of indecipherable tapping. Suddenly, it hits me. He doesn't know Morse. He's just banging away at random.

I slump against the wall and slide down to the floor, angry and frustrated. How are we to communicate if he doesn't know the code? I brood about this for a while. When it finally comes, the answer is so obvious I have to laugh. If my neighbor doesn't know Morse, I shall have to teach it to him.

Chapter Eight

Cat-and-Mouse

June 2, 1943. In the morning another inquisition at Gestapo headquarters. Then back to my cell, where I decide to begin my neighbor's Morse lessons. After banging the wall to get his attention, I carefully start sending the alphabet: dot-dash, dash-dot-dot-dot, dash-dot-dash-dot, dash-dot-dot—

My neighbor interrupts me with a flurry of banging.

Patiently, I begin again. Dot-dash, dash-dot-dot-dot—

More banging from next door.

Again I start over. Dot-dash, dash-dot-dot-dot—

Still more banging. Doesn't he realize what I'm trying to do? This could take weeks.

I take a deep breath. Dot-dash, dash-dot-dot-dot, dash-dot-dash-dot . . .

June 10, 1943. Life has settled into an awful routine. Every day I'm taken from my tiny cell at Fresnes to the Gestapo headquarters on Avenue Foch, where I'm questioned and beaten. When they get tired of beating me, they try to get me to talk by telling me how much they already know about underground operations. The idea is that I shouldn't feel bad about breaking down and confessing since they know everything anyway.

Sometimes my inquisitors are from the Abwehr, sometimes from the SD, sometimes from the Luftwaffe. Fortunately, they never work together. (Each of them seems to be convinced that the others are either incompetent or untrustworthy.) As a result, I can play one off against the other—satisfying the Abwehr man, for example, by "confessing" some information that I actually learned from his counterpart in the SD, and so on.

My Morse lessons are going slowly. My neighbor is a willing student, but his memory doesn't seem to be very good. I must have sent him the alphabet a thousand times already, and still he keeps sending it back wrong.

June 15, 1943. For the sake of my sanity, I've declared war on the fleas who inhabit the straw mattress in my cell. They are small and tough, almost impossible to catch, and even harder to squash. But I've learned how to get them—trapping and mashing the little beasts between the spoons the guards have given me for meals. My record so far is forty-seven in one hour. My goal is to break one hundred.

Unknown to Gaston while he languished in the Fresnes prison, London continued transmitting messages to and about Raymond as if he were still at large. For a time these transmissions made it seem as if Raymond had left the Perpignan area and returned to Grenoble. Later it appeared he was in Paris. Finally the underground passed the word that a POW had seen Raymond executed by the Gestapo along with a dozen or so other captured resistance workers. A marker was even erected to memorialize his death. Whether or not the Germans believed any of it, the detailed reports of Raymond's activities and death clearly contributed to their continuing uncertainty about Gaston's true identity.

July 7, 1943. Today's interrogation session is with the Abwehr man. He's a balding, middle-aged professional soldier who seems to know his business—by far the most intelligent of the lot.

Just beforehand, the guards leave me alone in a small room in the attic. There is a skylight in the roof a few feet over my head. Can this be my chance? Feebly, I leap for it. A few months ago I would have had no trouble at all scrambling out to freedom, but in my weakened state I might as well be jumping for the moon.

After several tries, I manage to grab hold of the skylight rim. I hang there helplessly, too weak to pull myself up and force the skylight open.

Finally, I hear the guards coming, and I drop back to the floor.

July 11, 1943. Up all night with stomach pains. Not only are the repeated beatings taking their toll, but I think the bad food—mainly coarse vegetables and dark bread—is giving me an ulcer. Killed seventy-seven fleas in one hour today. A new record.

July 19, 1943. Another flea-killing record—ninety-four in an hour. I'm certain to break one hundred before long.

July 25, 1943. My inquisitors are still trying to get me to admit that I'm Raymond. I, of course, continue to deny it. Are they beginning to believe me? I'm not sure that it even matters anymore. Our daily sessions have become a sort of ritual, in which we all play set parts in this elaborate game I've constructed. They badger and beat me; I feed them some information that I know they already have.

August 3, 1943. I've been thinking a lot about religion lately, about how much evil the Church has done over the centuries in the name of God. I suppose I've been influenced a lot by my father's atheism. Certainly, I share his contempt for what he used to call the Church's "comedy and hypocrisy"—its willingness to embrace dogma and meaningless ritual, the almost instinctive way it has of avoiding the hard truths of morality.

The Germans seem to understand this sort of hypocrisy very well. After all, they've used it to lure more than a few priests into their campaign against the Jews. Like the Church, the Germans talk about law and order, and they force people to live according to their rules. What's sad is how eagerly people embrace this kind of authoritarianism—the extent to which so many are unwilling (or unable) to come to grips with their own individual moral responsibility, the enthusiasm with which they take refuge in some big, powerful institution that says it has all the answers.

Yet none of this means there isn't some sort of higher power, does it? So many people in so many different places all over the world believe in a God. They can't all be wrong. Maybe there *is* some "force" out there.

But how do we learn to understand it? Is there just one way? Maybe we each have to find our own path. (This reminds me of those books on Sufism my old student Fonsy once lent me. What's become of him? I wonder.) Then again, if there are many paths to the truth, what does that say about the Castiaux family's sincere and altruistic Protestantism? Or Raymonde's Catholicism? Is there no real difference between their faiths—are they really no better or worse than anyone else's? Somehow, I can't believe that you can have it any way you want.

August 11, 1943. A great shock at Gestapo headquarters this morning. Whom did I pass in the hallway but Marcel Orset's wife, all dressed up and looking very nervous. That must mean they've arrested Marcel. Fortunately Mme. Orset didn't see me. The fact that Germans haven't tried to get her to identify me is an encouraging sign—maybe they really *are* beginning to believe that I'm not Raymond.

August 18, 1943. My twenty-second birthday. I dreamt last night that I was in my bedroom at home in Ghent. I was sitting on my bed, staring at the wallpaper that my father put up when I was very young. It covers three walls and tells a story. The first panel shows a little boy and girl driving down a garden path in a toy automobile. In the second panel, the auto has just run over a duckling. The third shows the boy looking back in sorrow at what he's done— while his auto heads straight for three more ducks. How often I have stared at the wallpaper and thought: If the boy doesn't stop looking back at the dead duck, he's going to kill another one.

Perhaps that's what the dream is telling me. Don't look back, look ahead. Instead of worrying about the mistakes of the past, I should be planning for the future.

Every day for the next four months, Gaston was taken into Paris to the Gestapo headquarters on the Avenue Foch to be questioned and beaten. In particular, the Germans were desperate for any information they could get out of him on where the long-rumored Allied

invasion of Europe would take place. Throughout it all, Gaston contin-
ued playing his little game of intellectual cat and mouse—taking
the facts he learned in one interrogation session and using them in
the next, twisting and distorting them, feeding them to his inquisitors
in tantalizing little pieces. It wasn't easy keeping it all straight in
his mind—which bits he had learned from which interrogators, whom
he had told what. He worried constantly that he would make a mistake,
that another captured agent would inadvertently betray him. Still,
he had no choice but to carry on. As long as the Germans believed
him to possess important information, they would keep him alive.

December 7, 1943. On the way back from what seems like my ten-
thousandth interrogation session, as the guards lead me across the
prison's main hall, I pass a familiar figure—a tall, thin man with
slicked-back dark hair. The man is standing next to a Gestapo officer.
He stares at me intently, and my stomach turns over. It's Adolphe
Manet—the agent from Toulouse whom Sabot and I had suspected
of being a double.

Quickly I turn my face to the wall. Too late. Manet has recognized
me. "Raymond!" he shouts. "It's me! Adolphe!"

I pretend not to know what he's talking about, but it's no use.
"That's him," Manet says to the Gestapo officer with him. "That's
the famous Raymond."

So it's over. After more than six months, the long game of cat
and mouse I've been playing with my inquisitors is finally finished.
In a way, I think I've won. At the very least, I've given my networks
more than enough time to protect themselves against anything the
Germans might learn from me.

At a signal from the officer standing with Manet, the guards drag
me outside and throw me into a Gestapo car. I'm driven back into
Paris, surrounded by silent, impassive SS men, wondering what they'll
do to me now. Torture me some more? To what end? Kill me?
Maybe.

I once read somewhere that human beings are constitutionally
incapable of conceiving of their own deaths—of really believing that
they're ever going to die. It must be true. I can accept the fact
that death is inevitable—indeed, I've been trying to live my life as

if it might come at any moment—but I can't really believe it's going to happen. Not now, at any rate. Not just yet.

At Gestapo headquarters on the Avenue Foch, I'm beaten savagely and methodically by four brawny guards for what seems like several hours. I can't really tell how long it goes on; I keep passing out. No one even bothers to question me. The Germans are simply angry that I managed to deceive them for so long, and they want some revenge.

Eventually, the guards leave me on the floor in the dark. I can barely move, but I'm still alive. That's a comforting thought. It means the Gestapo must feel there's more they can get out of me. And that means I have a chance to survive.

December 8, 1943. I'm awakened by a kick from a Gestapo guard. "Get up, you pig!" he shouts. "Now!"

It's early. Before seven, I'd guess. Painfully, I struggle to my feet. My entire body is sore, and my head feels as if it's swollen to twice its normal size.

The guard leads me to an office. Sitting behind the desk is a small, plump SD officer with a pasty face and the ratlike eyes of a professional cop. "Good morning, Raymond," he says. "Or is it Rinus?"

I blink uncomprehendingly. The officer smiles and shakes his head. "No need to play dumb," he says. "Not anymore. You don't think Adolphe Manet is our only informant, do you? Well, he's not. We also have the Jew John Cohen."

I try to look unconcerned—as if I don't know what he's talking about.

"Oh, yes," he continues, "we've got Cohen—along with many incriminating documents. He says that if we let him go, he will lead us to you. I suspect he'll be very disappointed when he finds out you're already in custody."

I stare at the German blankly. "Don't you understand?" he says, his voice low and soft, almost compassionate. "The Jew doesn't care about you. He is worried only about his own skin."

The officer peers at me, looking for some sign that he's getting through. I say nothing.

"You do not believe me?" he says, a trace of a smile flitting across his face. "I can show you the documents he kept in his apartment. He thought he could use them as bargaining chips if he got caught." He shakes his head and grimaces with professional distaste. "How can you trust such a man?"

I remain silent, but my insides are churning, my mind racing.

Betrayed by John? Impossible. He'd die first. The Germans must be bluffing.

But what about the documents they supposedly found in John's apartment? The officer must be telling the truth about that. Otherwise, he wouldn't have dared to offer to show them to me. And if John kept documents at home—which is against all the rules—who knows what else he might or might not have done?

I've got to stay calm. If the Germans were sure of their information, they wouldn't be so eager to have me confirm it. And as long as they're *not* sure, I'll have room to maneuver.

December 9, 1943. Once again I'm awakened early. This time the guard leads me to a rear courtyard, where I'm manacled and put in the back of a staff car. I sit there in dazed silence, shivering in the morning cold. After a few minutes, two Gestapo officers climb in on either side of me, and the car lurches into motion.

We head down the Avenue Foch, then eastward out of the city. At first I wonder if I'm being taken to some remote spot to be executed. But no, that doesn't make sense—if the Germans wanted to kill me, they would've done it at Gestapo headquarters.

After a while, the two Gestapo officers drift into conversation. I guess they don't know I can speak German myself. Or maybe they don't care. In any case, from what they say I manage to figure out that our destination is the Gestapo prison at The Hague—what we in the underground have nicknamed the Oranje Hotel.

December 10, 1943. My accommodations here at the Oranje Hotel leave a lot to be desired. It's an awful place, filthy and damp. They're keeping me by myself in a small holding cell. One of the guards tells me not to bother trying to get comfortable. I'm to be moved again tomorrow—this time, to the maximum-security prison at Haaren, a hundred kilometers southeast of here.

As I settle down for the night, a wonderful thought occurs to me: maybe the underground has gotten word that I've been transferred here from Fresnes. Maybe tomorrow, when I'm being driven to Haaren, they'll ambush the car and free me. Such things have happened before. Why shouldn't they happen again?

December 11, 1943. I spend the day alone in my cell. Finally, late in the afternoon, I'm put in another Gestapo car for the drive southeast to Haaren. It's cold and overcast—really gloomy weather—but I can scarcely contain my excitement. I'm going to be rescued. I'm sure of it.

We reach Haaren—without incident—just after dark. The prison here was once a monastery. Now it's illuminated by searchlights and surrounded by three concentric rings of barbed wire. I'm immediately brought upstairs to a wing of the building where the monks used to live. The guards lead me down a long corridor lined with what seem to be ordinary wooden doors, all of which have peepholes drilled through them at eye level. The peepholes are covered by small metal latches.

Finally, we arrive at what I assume is to be my cell. It's cold and damp and quite small. A narrow bunk is attached to one wall, a sink to another. There is one tiny window—a narrow, barred opening high in the wall opposite the door. A single, bare light bulb burns in the center of the ceiling. Something tells me I'm going to get to know this room very well indeed.

December 12, 1943. I'm up early, uncomfortable and disoriented by my new surroundings. Not much sleep last night. They kept turning on the light in my cell—in order to watch me through the peephole, I guess.

As I lean over the sink to wash my face, I hear a rhythmic surge of water in the pipes, as if someone in one of the cells is quickly opening and closing a faucet over and over again. The staccato rhythm sounds strangely familiar. Of course. It's Morse code. The prison grapevine.

I turn my head and listen carefully as the surges spell out the words: "W-h-o a-r-e y-o-u?"

The message is directed at me. I am debating whether or not to answer it when I hear a noise in the corridor. A moment later a guard flings open the door. He stares at me for a moment, then holds out an old safety razor and a tin cup containing perhaps an inch of soapy water. "Prisoners are permitted the privilege of shaving on Tuesdays and Fridays," he barks, as if quoting a regulation. "Today is Friday. You have two minutes."

I take the razor from him and walk to the sink. The guard stands in the doorway watching me—I suppose to make sure I won't try to slit my wrists or something. I run the razor over my cheek and wince. The blade is so dull I doubt I could open a vein with it even if I wanted to.

When the guard finally leaves, I turn my attention back to the grapevine. From what I can hear, it seems as if there are several dozen WIM agents with me at Haaren. I manage to get a few names before I'm interrupted once again, this time by a guard with my breakfast—coarse dark bread and thin gruel.

As I'm finishing it, another guard appears with some fresh clothes for me. He watches as I dress, then leads me out of my cell and down the long corridor.

The atmosphere seems strangely peaceful—like that of the monastery this place once was—the silence broken only by the hard slap of the guard's hobnail boots on the stone floor. There are no other prisoners in sight.

As we pass a line of closed cell doors, I find myself wondering what the inmates hidden behind them look like. Many are probably former agents of mine. Yet if the doors were suddenly to open, I'm sure I wouldn't recognize a single one. I know their code names, their backgrounds, their war records. But not their faces—nor they, mine.

At the end of the corridor we go down a flight of stairs, then along another corridor to a door marked "WIM." The guard opens the door and gestures for me to enter. I walk into a large room— an office, really—and stop, dumbstruck. Tacked up on the far wall, behind a massive desk, is a huge organizational chart, perhaps three meters high and four meters wide, labeled in large letters: "WIM DIENST" ("WIM Network").

At the top of the chart is a box marked "London." Just below it is another box, this one labeled "Rinus." And under that a forest of other boxes, some with names in them—the names of my sections.

In short, I am looking at a schematic representation of the entire WIM organization.

I've never seen anything like it. No one in WIM—or any underground organization—would dare to put something like this down on paper. Until this moment, I would have sworn that the only place this sort of detailed description existed was in my brain.

The sight is so shocking that I nearly panic. How can I possibly hope to protect what's left of WIM if the Gestapo knows so much about it? Why am I trying to hide little bits of information when they have the whole story? The questions reverberate in my mind; for a second I'm afraid I've actually blurted them out loud. Then I force myself to calm down. This could be nothing more than another Gestapo trick.

I begin to scan the chart methodically, trying to memorize the information contained on it. Almost immediately I realize there are many more blank boxes than ones with names in them. I also notice that some of the boxes with names in them have triangles in their upper right-hand corners—some black, some white. Others of the boxes are marked with a black cross, still others with another kind of symbol. I stare at the chart, trying to make sense of it.

Suddenly, I hear footsteps behind me. I turn to see a tall Gestapo officer standing in the doorway grinning at me triumphantly. "You were very clever," he says. "But as you can see, we already know almost everything."

He introduces himself as Hans Kramer, deputy to Col. Joseph Schreieder, chief of Gestapo counterintelligence in Holland. Kramer sits down behind the desk and shakes his head in what I suppose he means to be a fatherly way. "It's senseless for you to keep lying to us," he tells me. "England is lost. You have nothing more to fight for."

He gazes at me earnestly, but I don't reply.

"You were misled from the very beginning, you know," he continues. "The French let you and the other Belgians do their fighting for them, while they hid behind their fortresses and their armor. Once our Panzer divisions cut through their lines, they ran like pigs. The great French army fell in less than a week. *A week, Vandermeerssche!* They are pitiful, I tell you. No one fought better or harder than the Belgians. And for what?"

He shakes his head again. "It's the Jews, you know, who own their banks and their newspapers. The British, too. You should be fighting for your own people, for the freedom of Belgium. We are your real allies, your real friends—not them."

How many times have I heard this before from German interrogators? These "friends" have been beating and torturing me for more than six months. For all I know, they may even have killed my parents and sister. I stop listening and look around the office. It must have been a classroom once, with a high ceiling and a wall lined with large windows.

Through the windows, past the barbed wire and the soldiers with their machine guns, I can see a mature forest with tall trees, their branches naked and forlorn in the cold December drizzle. This will not be a pleasant place to spend the winter.

"It's senseless, I tell you!" Kramer suddenly exclaims, interrupting my reverie. I stare at him in surprise. He seems to be getting genuinely worked up. "All I want from you is the information. I am a professional. I have a job to do. You tell me what I want to know, and I will treat *you* like a professional. If you don't, I will be forced to resort to whatever measures are necessary. You must understand—many lives are at stake here. German lives. Belgian lives. Dutch lives. You can make things much easier on yourself and everyone else if you cooperate."

He looks at me expectantly. "Have you nothing to say?" he asks.

I shrug. We might as well establish the ground rules. "You're a professional and I'm not," I tell him. "You know how old I am and everything else about me. How could I possibly have done so much in such a short time? Who'd have given me that kind of responsibility? I've tried to help you, but—"

"I have your records, Vandermeerssche!" Kramer shouts back angrily. "I know how you lied to the others! You will not get away with that here! You will be made to understand whom you are dealing with!" He gestures to the guard standing behind me and barks, "Take him away!"

On the way back to my cell, I try to visualize the chart on Kramer's wall, trying to figure out what all the symbols stand for. Obviously, the boxes with names in them represent sections that have been identified by the Gestapo. (With a surge of relief, I recall how many of the boxes are blank—WIM is still a long way from being smashed.)

Now what about the triangles? Perhaps they signify that the Germans know more than just the name of the section—the identities of agents as well.

Then it hits me. In one of the boxes marked with a black triangle, I recognized the name of a section leader of ours who I know was picked up by the Gestapo. So the black triangles must indicate networks whose agents have been arrested. No doubt the black crosses mean the agents have been executed.

For the first time since I arrived here I have a sense of real hope. Thanks to the German obsession with organizing and documenting everything, I have something to work with. I can use the information on the chart to play cat and mouse with my inquisitors here, just as I did at Fresnes. I wonder if Kramer realizes what a useful tool he's given me. I must study his chart every chance I get—until I know it even better than he does.

December 15, 1943. The routine here seems slightly easier than that at Fresnes. I'm waked every morning around six by the sound of the guards stomping up and down the corridors, shouting at the prisoners to wash themselves. A few minutes later my door is flung open, and my clothes are tossed in to me. (The guards collect our clothes every evening; I suppose they feel no one would try to escape in his nightshirt.)

Around 6:30 the food cart comes rattling down the hall, bringing the mush that we're supposed to regard as breakfast. My stomach is in such bad shape that I find it better to eat a dry bread crust— or nothing at all.

After breakfast there's nothing for me to do but sit on my bunk and prepare for my daily session with Kramer. On weekday mornings, the guard comes to take me downstairs around 10:30. On weekends, I sit alone in my cell all day. I'm not permitted to read or write, to sing or whistle, to even see another prisoner. Occasionally, they take me outside for a little exercise—a short walk in a closed-off area behind the building.

The sessions with Kramer are grueling, but the strain is all mental. He tries to cajole me into cooperating, while I feed him information from his own chart. No beatings so far.

December 25, 1943. My first Christmas in prison. The guards mark the occasion by letting me have a slice of white bread for supper. It's the first white bread I've seen in months.

January 6, 1944. Things may be easier physically here at Haaren, but psychologically the strain is much greater. For one thing, Kramer's questioning is far more intensive—more subtle and persistent—than any I've encountered so far. For another, I'm still in solitary. For whatever reason, the Germans seem to be going to great lengths to make sure I have no contact whatsoever with any of the other prisoners. The corridor is always empty when I'm taken down to Kramer's office, and on several occasions the guards bringing me meals have slammed my door shut to keep me from even catching a glimpse of anyone else.

As a result, I spend most of my waking hours on my bunk daydreaming, conserving my energy for my daily bout with Kramer. So often—too often—I find myself thinking about my parents and sister, how I never managed to let them know how much I love them. This is the real torture.

Fortunately, I've learned to turn off my thoughts, to slow my mind and body to an almost semiconscious state, at the same time remaining alert for the slightest sound—such as the footsteps of a guard in the corridor or the signaling of the prison grapevine over the water pipes.

The grapevine helps keep me sane, but I'm wary of using it too much. Like any gossip mill, it's filled with rumors, distortions, and false information. More important, you never know who might be listening in. One slip, and all these weeks and months of fencing with the Germans could be wiped out.

That's the thing I must never let myself forget: We are playing for keeps here. A single mistake could cost me my life—or the lives of the people who trusted me.

January 18, 1944. I've discovered that I have a cellmate—a small, gray spider who lives under the sink. I've been watching him (or is it a her?) carefully, studying the way in which he stalks the unlucky flies that fall into his web.

The spider approaches his prey cautiously. Once he's sure that the victim is firmly caught, he attacks from behind, killing the fly slowly and deliberately, then sucking out its body fluids until nothing remains but an empty shell hanging in the web.

As killers go, the spider is quite calculating and efficient. But not, I think, as cruel as the Gestapo.

Unfortunately for the spider, there don't seem to be many flies about—the result, I guess, of the evil-smelling disinfectant the guards use to wash down the floors. How typical of the Germans to make life miserable even for the bugs.

Gaston's daily battle of wits with Kramer continued through the winter and early spring. It was a grim and demoralizing experience. As a result of Englandspiel, *the hugely successful Gestapo counterintelligence operation through which the Germans managed to both monitor and control all radio traffic between London and the Dutch underground, Kramer was able to taunt Gaston with his detailed knowledge not only of resistance operations in the Netherlands but of personnel and procedures at SOE headquarters in London.*

Gaston thought often about escape—not so much as a realistic possibility, but more as a mental exercise to help him get through the bleak days and long nights. The fact was, the Germans never left him alone or unwatched for a minute. It wouldn't have mattered much if they had. All those months of beatings and bad food had taken their toll: Even had he been given the chance to run, Gaston was too weak to have gotten very far.

May 10, 1944. It's a year today since I was arrested in Perpignan. How long ago that seems. From the rumors circulating on the grapevine, it sounds as if it's only a matter of time before the Reich crumbles. But one never knows. Hope is a dangerous thing. It can sustain you, but it also can drive you mad.

For the past few days the weather's been warm and sunny. I lie on my bunk staring up at the ceiling, focusing my eyes on the tiny particles of dust floating in the shaft of sunlight that streams in through my small window. The dust motes reflect the light like miniscule planets in a universe millions of miles away.

I imagine myself one of those motes, floating up that shaft of sunlight and out the barred window, being borne aloft by the wind over the carefully groomed Dutch countryside, over the intricate system of dikes and canals and windmills the Dutch use to irrigate their land. The tulips have long since bloomed, but there must be petunias and pansies and yellow-and-white narcissus in the fields and window boxes. How peaceful and relaxing it is to share the quiet beauty of this country, even if I am just a speck of dust floating in the breeze.

Chapter Nine

On Trial

May 16, 1944. I've been thinking about religion again. Maybe the thing to do is to try out all the different religions and see what happens. I wonder if I can remember how you do a Rosary.

May 24, 1944. Summer is coming. I find myself lying on my bunk, staring for hours out at the small patch of sky visible through my tiny window, hoping to catch a glimpse of a bird. Occasionally, I see a swallow—or a seagull soaring inland in search of a freshly plowed field and a change in diet.

I wonder about the monks who occupied this cell when Haaren was still a monastery. What were they like? What did they think about? I doubt they spent much time staring out the window, dreaming of freedom. They could walk out the door and wander through the forest any time they wanted.

Probably, they weren't interested in going anywhere. For them, I suppose, freedom was to be found in the service of God. Lucky them.

June 4, 1944. Today marks exactly three years since I left home. I find myself overwhelmed with worry about my family. Have they been betrayed, arrested by the Nazis? Are they suffering because of my work in the underground? I've got to know. No matter what it takes, I must survive so I can find out.

June 8, 1944. Scientist that I am, I've decided to systemize my thoughts on religion in an orderly fashion. I've come to the following conclusions:

1. The religious experience seems to be universal—in different forms, it has existed at all times in the history of mankind, in all parts of the world.

2. Based on my experience with and observations of so-called natural phenomena, it's clear that there must be forces at work that are greater and more complicated than we as human beings can ever fully understand.

3. Nonscientists refer to these forces by all kinds of names—the most common of which is God.

4. Lacking a better term, I see nothing wrong with using the term God myself. But I refuse to accept the dogma of any religion.

5. Though the intelligence of human beings is too limited to grasp the full nature of what they call God, it is an observable fact that prayer (whether uttered by a Sufi, a Jew, a Christian, or whatever) does help individuals to cope with life and even overcome certain difficulties.

This, then, is the sense in which I believe in God and the power of prayer.

June 12, 1944. Rumors are circulating that the Allies have landed somewhere in France and are pushing east. Can this be true?

I continue to take each day as it comes. It's the only way I know to survive. And I intend to survive. I must.

June 15, 1944. Lying on my bunk recovering from my latest session with Kramer, I hear a strange droning noise coming from somewhere outside the prison. It grows louder and louder, until there's no mistaking what it is—the angry growling of aircraft engines.

I sit up and cock my ear. This isn't the whine of the Luftwaffe's Stukas, it's the throaty roar of heavy bombers—the Flying Fortresses of the American air force!

A moment later the bombs start falling. I can feel the tremors even through the thick walls and floors.

They're getting closer. Soon the doors and beds are shaking. Pandemonium is breaking loose. I can hear the prisoners in the other cells, shouting and singing—as if they believe the pilots might hear them.

The guards race up and down the corridors, kicking the cell doors, shouting: "Ruhe! Ruhe! Sei still! Sei still!" But the shouting only grows louder as the planes and their bombs come ever nearer. It's as if the bombers are homing in on our voices.

Are we so crazy for freedom that we want the bombs to drop right on top of us? Maybe. It's the first real sign of hope any of us has had in months.

I'm awakened around midnight by the scream of air-raid sirens. Another attack. The Allies must really be pounding the area. Perhaps the end of the war really is at hand.

July 1, 1944. There's been Allied bombing nearly every day for the last two weeks. At our daily sessions together, Kramer seems nervous and distracted.

July 10, 1944. The heat is oppressive. As if to compensate, rumors are flying that we will soon be liberated. They say the Allies are racing east at breakneck speed.

July 19, 1944. Kramer's attitude is different today. He seems angry and frustrated, desperate in a way I've never seen before. For the first time, I'm filled with a sense of foreboding.

"I repeat it now for the last time!" he shouts at me at the beginning of our session. "This is your last chance! The English are fools. We have beaten them at every step. We control their agents and their radio transmissions. We tell London when to drop their agents and where to drop them—and then we arrest them as soon as they touch the ground. They're all here in Haaren, you know. Plenty of them."

I stare at Kramer. What is he talking about?

He rages on, obviously out of control. "The game is over, Vandermeerssche! We know everything! You might as well try to save yourself. You've done well to keep it up this long. No one else could have held out the way you have. I admire your bravery, but there's no point anymore. You think these dumb Englanders appreciate what you are trying to do for them? You think they would do the same for you? Of course not. It's time for you to start thinking about saving yourself."

He points to the WIM chart on his wall. "You built up a large organization, but you don't have to die with it. So why don't you cooperate? There's no hope for you if you don't, you know. We're professionals here, Vandermeerssche. You're just an amateur, hardly more than a boy. You put up a good fight, but the game is over and you've lost. So why don't you make the best of it? Your life is in your hands. After today, there's nothing more I can do for you."

With that, he dismisses me. Back in my cell, I sit on my bunk brooding about his bizarre new attitude. It was as if he'd finally given up, conceded me the game we've been playing all these months.

Then again, you never know with these Germans. They could take all the WIM agents out tomorrow morning and shoot them. Nothing would surprise me.

I'm awakened from a late-afternoon nap by what sounds like the food cart clattering down the corridor. Odd. It's not nearly time for supper.

I can hear other cell doors being opened and closed. Finally, the cart reaches my cell. The guard flings open the door and hands me a razor and a cup of soapy water. I stare at him in astonishment. We're getting shaves? On a Wednesday?

I try to see out into the corridor, but the guard stands in the way and barks, "Razieren!" Obediently, I move back to the sink and begin the painful process of shaving with the prison-issue razor. Today's blade seems even duller than usual.

As I shave, I try to make sense of this odd turn of events. The Allied bombings, Kramer's strange behavior, the rumors of a landing in France, and now this unprecedented break in the prison's previously inviolate routine—they all must add up to something. But what?

I hand the shaving utensils back to the guard, who places them back on his cart—carefully arranging and counting his supply of razors and tin cups. It's as if his life depended on keeping everything strictly in order and according to the rules. In a way, I suppose it does. Suddenly, I feel sorry for him.

When he leaves I sit back down on my bunk. Through my small

window I can see the evening sunlight beginning to fade. I must start preparing myself for tomorrow. Despite everything, I still have to figure out my next moves in the game.

I'm going over what Kramer said to me this morning when I hear a familiar sound from the pipes. I move to the sink, and listen as the grapevine transmits the words: "T-o-m-o-r-r-o-w W-I-M a-g-e-n-t-s g-o o-n t-r-i-a-l."

So the game with Kramer really is finished. No need now to go over where the pieces were left the last time. I sit down on my bunk. Judging from the faint light visible through my window, it could just as easily be dawn as dusk. Funny how you have to work so hard in prison just to keep track of time.

July 20, 1944. After breakfast, the guard opens my door and orders me out into the corridor. To my astonishment, it's filled with prisoners. I can't believe it. It's been so long since I've seen anyone but guards and Gestapo officers.

There must be fifty prisoners standing in line—all, I assume, WIM agents, though I don't recognize any of them. I feel like hugging each man and asking his code name. Instead, I take my place in line without showing any emotion.

As I do, the prisoners begin to murmur to each other.

"That's Rinus!"

"There's the chief!"

"Look at him! He seems so young!"

I can't help but smile.

The guards march us down the corridor, then down the stairs to a first-floor assembly room I've never seen before. Outside the door, two soldiers are sitting at a small table. One of them, an Austrian with pale eyes and a sad face, calls out my name. I step forward, and the other one hangs around my neck a piece of cardboard with a large "1" written on it.

From inside the assembly room, I hear an officer call out, "Nummer Eins! Hereinkommen!"

I enter. The room is spacious and bright, with large windows and high ceilings. A lone officer is sitting at a long table at the far end of the room. The table is flanked by the black flags of the Gestapo, with their sinister death's-head insignia. On the wall behind the

table is a huge Nazi flag, topped by a large imperial German eagle.
In front of the table, filling the room in neat rows like a theater,
are fifty empty chairs. The officer points to the first row, and I take
the seat nearest the window.

The officer looks back to the door and orders "Nummer Zwei" to
come in. Number two turns out to be John Cohen. I stare at him
intently as he walks toward me. He returns my gaze with hard,
expressionless eyes, then looks away. I wonder if he really did offer
to betray me to the Germans—and, if so, what he's told them about
WIM.

The officer continues to call off numbers, but I don't recognize
any of the other agents. I study their faces, looking for some familiar
sign. But without their code names, they're all strangers to me.

Suddenly, I begin to smile. Except for John, I don't recognize
anyone! Rosa, the butcher's wife from Antwerp, the chief contact
for all the Dutch couriers—she's not here. Max, the Dutchman who
heads one of our largest networks—I don't see him either. They
may have caught some of us, but only some. WIM survives.

I wonder if any of the others realize this. Probably not. I deliberately
organized WIM in such a way that no one but me would really
know its true size. For example, I gave some of my section chiefs
code names, while others are identified by code numbers. I've inter-
mixed them to make it impossible for anyone to figure out how
many units and subdivisions we have. There is a division 10 and a
division 12 and a division 16, but is there also an 11, a 13, 14, or
15? I'm the only one who knows.

Before long the room is filled with prisoners. Suddenly, the guards
shout, "Achtung!" We all stand up. A Luftwaffe general strides into
the room and marches up to the table. He cuts an impressive figure,
resplendent in a blue uniform with gold epaulets and a high-peaked
cap that makes him look seven feet tall. A nasty dueling scar runs
down his right cheek in a straight line from eye to mouth. Two
Luftwaffe captains follow him; then come the prosecutor, a translator,
and two typists.

With great ceremony, the general takes off his cap and lays it on
the table. Then he removes his white gloves and lays them across
the crown of his cap. That done, he pulls out a chair and sits down.
His aides follow suit.

A moment later two soldiers in the midnight-black uniform of the Gestapo carry in two large boxes labeled "Feld Gericht." So the Gestapo is turning over its intelligence records for a Luftwaffe field trial. The Germans must want to get this over with quickly and without complications. The Luftwaffe is notorious for conducting merciless inquiries in which few prisoners ever escape the death penalty.

Framed by the big Nazi flag on the wall behind them, sitting at the long table in their fine tailored uniforms, the Luftwaffe general and his aides look larger than life. The Germans certainly know how to put on a show.

At a nod from the general, the prosecutor stands up to begin the proceedings. He is a swarthy man with bushy eyebrows and an angry expression. "The accused are guilty of the most heinous crimes against the Third Reich," he screeches. "They are a gang of Jews, Communists, intellectuals, and vagabonds who have conspired to oppose the German occupation. They have caused the death of innocent women and children. They have aided the enemy in directing strikes against the Wehrmacht."

With each word, the prosecutor grows more enraged, jabbing an accusing finger at us as he spits out each new charge. It's an amazing performance. You'd think we were the only ones fighting the war—and you'd never know that not one of us ever used a gun or committed a single act of sabotage. If words could kill, this man would be a mass murderer.

Finally, the prosecutor sits down, out of breath, wiping his forehead with a white handkerchief. The general looks out at us. "Now we will give you a chance to answer the charges against you," he says. "Eins, aufstehe!"

As I stand up, the guards march the other prisoners out of the room. Obviously, they don't want the others to hear the court's questions—or to see how I answer them.

When the room is clear, the prosecutor begins reading the specific charges against me. The indictment is long and complicated, but it boils down to this: As the organizer of an intelligence network that transmitted vital information to the enemy, I am considered responsible for the deaths of thousands of good and loyal German soldiers.

When the prosecutor finishes, the general opens a folder and consults a sheaf of papers, then fixes me with a penetrating stare. "Did you know that the agent John wanted to betray you?" he asks me. "Did you know that you were betrayed from the beginning by your London contacts?"

It's ridiculous. The Gestapo asked me the same questions in Paris a year ago. These people don't know anything.

A feeling of triumph begins to rise inside me. I know there's no way I can escape being convicted of these trumped-up charges. But for the past year I've lived with the fear that either through weakness or carelessness I might have given something or someone away during one of my daily interrogation sessions. The inanity of the court's questions is proof that I haven't—that I've unquestionably won my game of cat and mouse.

"I started and then continued doing this work because I wanted to do the right thing for my country," I tell the general. "From what you and your colleagues tell me, I guess I did my job pretty well. That makes me proud. I have no regrets. My conscience is clear."

I'm ordered to sit down, and John is brought in. The prosecutor reads off the charges against him. They're as heavy-handed and over-blown as the ones against me. If John really was a collaborator (and I'm beginning to doubt it), he certainly hasn't gotten anything for his trouble.

After John, seven other agents are called in, one after the other, to hear the individual charges against them. Bored, I look out the window. The sun has dropped below the trees. A group of guards is marching along a gravel path that circles the prison, singing on their way to evening mess. The Germans do love to sing.

Eventually, the general glances up at the large clock on the wall. It's past six. Without a word, he closes his folder and stands up. His fellow officers quickly gather up their papers and follow him out of the court.

After they're gone, the guards march us out. I'm pleased with the way things have gone. Of course this trial is to be a mockery, an absurd ritual performed by professional killers who want some sort of token justification for their acts. But we have all kept our pride and dignity. No one broke down or gave anything away.

On the way back to the cells, I hear the other prisoners whispering the latest rumors.

"The Americans and the British are putting up a terrific fight."

"They'll be here in a few days."

"They have six lawyers working to get us out of here."

"The Dutch government in London has offered to exchange some German prisoners for us."

"They've sent a million guilders by parachute to set Rinus free."

The sight of so many WIM agents in the same room together has obviously raised everyone's spirits. I just hope no one gets too carried away with optimism. Rumors are dangerous like that. They lift you up—but if (as is so often the case) they turn out to be false, they can plummet you into despair.

To my surprise, the guards take me to a new cell. Even more surprising, there's another prisoner in it—a young, aristocratic-looking Dutchman who introduces himself as Jan. Jan is in his mid-twenties with an open, intelligent face and closely cropped blonde hair.

"I know who you are," he says. "You're Rinus, the chief of the WIM group. I understand you're a Belgian. And so young!" He babbles on about how grateful he is for what I've tried to do for his country, how much he admires me, how he wishes he'd been able to accomplish half as much as I did. He claims to have been active in the underground for only two months before being arrested. "Please," he asks, "tell me more about what you did."

Needless to say, I'm immediately suspicious. Jan is either a painfully naive young man or an incredibly clumsy double agent—perhaps both. After all, why else would the Germans have given me a cell-mate—my first in all these months—if not in an effort to get more information out of me?

Then, again, perhaps they're worried that I might try to kill myself if left alone. Men facing death do strange things, and the Germans hate it when a prisoner beats them to the punch like that.

Without saying anything to Jan, I lie down on the bunk and close my eyes. It's been an exhausting day. Even if I had the patience and inclination, I simply don't have the energy to answer his questions.

"I suppose you feel you can't trust me," Jan says after a bit. "I don't expect you to tell me anything that might harm you or anyone else. Can't we talk about your philosophy and your beliefs? You see, I can't understand how so many of my countrymen can bow and scrape the way they do in front of the Germans. Why should it take a foreigner, a Belgian, to lead our resistance efforts?"

I open my eyes but don't reply. Jan stares at me for a moment, then looks away, embarrassed. I feel a little sorry for him. "Forgive me for not speaking much," I finally say. "It's been a very long day for me, and I'm just tired. We can discuss such weighty subjects some other time."

We undress in silence and climb into our bunks. The guard comes in a few minutes later to collect our clothes and turn off the light. In the darkness, Jan calls out, "Good night, Rinus. Good luck."

Before long I hear Jan's breathing subside into the slow and even cadences of sleep. Only someone with a clear conscience—or no conscience at all—could drop off so easily. It seems strange to be sharing a room with someone after all this time. Especially someone who asks so many questions.

July 21, 1944. I'm awakened by the sound of the cell door being flung open. It's the guard giving us our clothing for the day. I've been dreaming about home, about working in my father's shop as a small boy—of the rich, clean smell of freshly cut wood, and the sharp, pungent odor of the stains, oil, and varnish used to finish it.

I find it strange getting dressed with someone else in the room. Fortunately, Jan respects my silence, allowing me to collect my thoughts about the coming day's trial.

Immediately after breakfast the guards come to take me back downstairs. "Good luck," Jan whispers as they lead me out. "Have courage."

The WIM prisoners seem quiet and subdued this morning, though as we approach the trial room I hear them exchanging rumors.

"It looks like only a few will get the death sentence . . ."

"They say the Allies have landed in Jutland and are moving south . . ."

"The British are bombing Germany every night. It can't last much longer . . ."

The proceedings are much the same as yesterday's. Agent after agent is called in to be read the same outrageous charges and asked the same stupid questions. My mind wanders, and I find myself thinking of the collaborators who had betrayed so many of us. It fills me with rage. What kind of world is it in which the jackals who betray their countrymen for money can grow fat and run free, while the real patriots and freedom fighters are caged and killed like animals?

With an effort of will, I turn my attention back to the trial—just in time to see the prosecutor call in a prisoner I recognize. It's little Henk, an agent who worked for us in the Breda area. Henk was a photography expert. He would stay up all night in his makeshift lab, converting piles of documents to microfilm—then spend the next day scouring the town for the chemicals he needed, making his way from one pharmacy to the next, never buying too much from one source lest he raise anyone's suspicions.

As little Henk approaches the table at the front of the room, it's clear that the months in a Gestapo prison have taken their toll on him. One of his shoulders sags, and he walks with a limp. But he's all right. I can see the fire and hatred in his eyes as the prosecutor reads the charges against him.

After finishing with Henk, the tribunal breaks for lunch. Even the prosecutor seems to be getting tired of having to repeat the long list of charges against each agent. The Luftwaffe officers make a big deal of shuffling their papers and pretending to check the facts of each case, but their questions are increasingly disjointed and often redundant.

I can't understand why the Germans are bothering to go to all this trouble. They can't be concerned about legal niceties. If they were, they'd have provided us with legal counsel as the Geneva Convention requires.

As we're being marched out of the trial room, one of the prisoners asks the court translator how it looks for us. The translator glances around to make sure all the officers are gone, then whispers: "The verdict will fall within a week. They say that thirteen of you will be condemned to die. The rest will get prison terms."

The news quickly ripples through the line, and a fresh crop of rumors springs up.

"Only thirteen will get the death penalty—and even they may not have to die!"

"We're going to be freed! The Germans are worried about their own necks now!"

"The Americans and the British will hang the Gestapo killers!"

"The Allies have landed in Denmark and are coming down from the north!"

I don't like this kind of wild talk. The key to survival is tight mental discipline. You've got to believe that you're going to make it—that, despite everything, you're going to walk out of here one day. But you can't torture yourself worrying about just when that's going to happen. You've got to take each day as it comes, recognizing that every time you make it through another twenty-four hours, you've achieved a victory—you've come that much closer to the day when you'll finally be liberated.

The pace of the trial seems to speed up after lunch. The remaining agents are brought in quickly, and the questions seem more perfunctory than ever. Obviously, the Germans think they've numbered us in order of our importance in WIM. They were right about the first few—me and John and some of the others. But after that, it's clear they've just been guessing.

At first I feel a bit sorry for the lesser agents who've had the misfortune to be numbered among the first thirteen. But then I begin to smell yet another German trick. The translator must have been instructed to say what he did. Otherwise, he wouldn't have dared open his mouth. The plan is obvious: You pass the word that only some of the prisoners are going to be condemned, then sit back and wait for the weaker ones to crack. It's one of the Gestapo's favorite tactics—to try to split a group and pit one member against the next.

By the time the tribunal finishes with the last agent, the sun is low in the sky. The general puts his hands on the table in front of him and stares out at us. Then, slowly, he closes his folders and places them neatly in a stack. That done, he rises and puts on his gloves, carefully straightening the seams on each finger. Finally, he places his peaked cap on his head and stands there, an imposing figure in his splendid uniform, obviously ready to make some sort of pronouncement.

"The verdict," he says, "will be delivered tomorrow. The session will start in the afternoon."

With that, he turns on his heel and walks out. The other officers follow in his wake.

The men are quiet and subdued as we're marched back to our cells. No more excited whispers, no rumors. Tomorrow we shall know our fate.

Unlike the others, I feel a real sense of triumph, almost joy. A group is only as strong as its weakest member, and no one had cracked. No one broke down. No one betrayed the organization. Outside, around the country, throughout the occupied territories, WIM is still in business. The holes left by those of us who've been arrested have been—or will be—filled by others. We have not been beaten. Even better, time is on our side. The longer we can hold out, the more likely it is that we will win.

Back in my new cell, I find Jan reading a small copy of the New Testament that he's managed to smuggle into the prison. He jumps up as I come in, filled with questions. "How did it go? Did they sentence you today? Did anyone confess?"

I sit down on my bunk, exhausted.

"Today you must talk to me," Jan insists. "I can't stand not knowing what is happening anymore. This place depresses me so much. If only I could get out of here for one last mission. I'd like to die fighting the Germans, instead of rotting here in this cell. Rinus, please! Talk to me!"

I shake my head and smile. "Calm down," I tell him. "Save your energy. You'll need it."

Jan blushes in embarrassment, then apologizes for his outburst. To spare his feelings, I change the subject and ask him about his Bible.

"Reading it gives me strength," he says. "I've chosen a passage for you. I assume you're a Catholic."

I start to explain about my problems with the Church. We wind up talking for hours about religion and theology. Finally, Jan reads me the passage he's chosen for me. It's from Romans: "If God be with us, who can be against us?"

Jan looks at me earnestly. "God is with you, Rinus, even though you may not know him or believe in him as I do. The Germans cannot touch you. They cannot change what you've created. We will fight on."

I'm touched by his words, but I can barely keep my eyes open. Jan apologizes for keeping me up so long and sits there watching me as I fall asleep.

July 22, 1944. I have to shake Jan to get him up when the guards come by with our clothing. He must have been up half the night thinking.

Jan's a good person, but it's probably just as well the Gestapo caught him as quickly as it did, before he could be accused of doing anything serious. I doubt he'd last very long under torture, and he's too proud to bear the humiliation of breaking. He'd wind up a suicide for sure.

Soon after breakfast the grapevine starts up with a vengeance. There's a lot of talk about how field trials almost always mean the death penalty, and about how you know when your time has come: the guard puts a cardboard cover over your window, so when they come to get you just before dawn the light from your cell doesn't violate the blackout. There's also talk about the Germans' increasing desperation, how they're getting nervous about leaving any survivors who could talk about atrocities or violations of international law.

It's the sort of rumormongering that doesn't do anyone any good. I wait for a pause in the stream, then put through a simple message of my own: "You must worry about only one thing—be strong in front of the Germans."

With that, I lie back on my bunk and try to ignore the frantic signaling. The Germans were clever to schedule the sentencing for the afternoon. They obviously knew rumors would be flying all morning, that the tension would build until it was nearly unbearable.

Somehow, I know I'm going to make it. I just wish I could convince the others that they will too. If they believe they are, they'll have the strength to survive.

We're brought downstairs just after lunch. The men seem to be in slightly better spirits—at the very least, relieved that the debilitating uncertainty is finally about to end.

Through the trial-room window I can see the members of the tribunal walking along the gravel path. The atmosphere this afternoon seems strangely benign, almost friendly—the guards joking with one another, the prisoners taking their regular seats, chatting away as if here to see a movie or a play. Perhaps what we've just been through was only a pretrial; perhaps today won't be the end for any of us. According to the latest rumor, Allied troops have landed near Hamburg.

The gossiping ceases as the tribunal members stride in and take their places at the large table. All is quiet for a moment. Then, unexpectedly, there's a shout from the back: "Oh, my God!"

Every head in the room swings around. A pair of Gestapo guards are marching in with two women—each the wife of a WIM agent.

For a moment there's silence. What are these women doing here? None of us knew they'd even been arrested. Despite the presence of the tribunal, the room fills with the buzz of shocked whispering.

"What's going on?"

"Can they bring in more people so late in the trial?"

"Is the trial going to start all over again?"

With a crack like a pistol shot, the general slaps the table with the flat of his hand. "Ordnung!" he shouts angrily.

The buzz subsides.

The charging and questioning of the women take only a minute or two, after which they're ordered to sit in the back of the room.

Then the prosecutor gets up to make his closing statement.

"We have proven," he says, gazing about malevolently, "that these prisoners are a well-organized gang of Jews, Bolsheviks, and intellectuals who have plotted against the Wehrmacht and the German government. They are responsible for countless acts of sabotage. They have given information to the enemy about military operations and troop movements and have helped him plan his bombings of German cities, causing the deaths of thousands of innocent women and children. They have broken German law and the laws of the occupation forces. They are traitors and must be treated as such. They must serve as an example to others who would plot against the fatherland and the Führer."

The prosecutor mops his brow, then straightens up. "Germany will live!" he shouts. "Germany will always live!" He turns to face the tribunal. "There is only one punishment adequate for them. Death to these criminals. Death to these enemies of the Third Reich!"

The general stares out at us impassively for a long moment, as if to give the prosecutor's words time to sink in. Then, slowly and deliberately, he begins reading from a small piece of paper.

The two women who were brought in at the last moment, he says, are to be released. One of the photographers—who was only "helping with the espionage"—is to have the specifications against him reduced. The rest of us are guilty of all charges.

It's insane. The verdict means that nearly all of us—not just thirteen, but forty-seven agents—are facing a death sentence. It's so typically German. Obviously, they've been planning this all along, perhaps even laughing about it as they anticipated the shocked looks on our faces.

The general folds up the piece of paper with the verdicts on it. He stares out at us for a moment, then announces that each prisoner will now be given an opportunity to say something to appeal both the verdict and the sentence that goes along with it. He will listen to our arguments and render a final decision tomorrow.

As the leader of WIM, I am to speak first. I must set a good example. The others will take their cue from me. I stand up and gaze evenly at the tribunal. I'm sure they won't give me much time to speak, so I'd better make my words count.

"I have no regrets about my actions," I begin. "On the contrary, based on what you have told me yourself, I am proud and pleased that I seem to have succeeded so well in defending my country and the freedom that you have taken from us. I am also proud to have worked with such fine and courageous people as I see around me here."

I turn my back on the tribunal and face the men. "Long live Holland!" I shout. "Long live Belgium!"

Enraged, the general barks an order, and a guard throws me back into my seat.

John is the next to speak. "This entire trial is illegal," he says. "It is a mockery of justice and humanity. The articles of the Geneva Convention require that we be provided with legal counsel and the means to defend ourselves. Yet we have been denied the opportunity to have a lawyer and a legal defense. To respond to your charges is to participate in an outrageous violation of human rights. There will be a record of this trial somewhere after you have lost the war, and you will be tried as war criminals. We are not afraid of cowards like you!"

John sits down and another agent is called up—then another, and another. Most keep their remarks short, and everyone is contemptuous of the Germans. A few refuse to speak at all. It is turning out better than I had hoped. Adriaan, a modest, soft-spoken pharmacist who is the picture of the correct Dutchman, is typical. "I'm really impressed by what you say I did," he tells the tribunal, "and I have only one regret. Knowing now that I am condemned to die, I'm only sorry I didn't do much more."

The men are quiet as we file out of the trial room. In the corridor outside my cell, the Austrian guard pulls me aside.

"I can't believe it," he whispers in a shocked voice. "What a terrible war this is. They are butchers and madmen. They treat all of us like animals who live only to be slaughtered." To my astonishment, he bursts into tears. "Both my sons were killed at the Russian front," he says. "They won't be satisfied until we're all dead."

I tell him to stop crying before one of the other guards reports him and he gets into trouble. "I'm sorry about your sons," I add.

This is madness. I'm facing the death penalty, and here I am comforting an enemy soldier.

Back in the cell, Jan is equally shocked. "Why even bother with a trial?" he asks, after I tell him of the verdict. "Why not just take everyone out and shoot them?"

It's a good question. Perhaps the "trial" was just one more step in the interrogation process. Or perhaps the Germans were just entertaining themselves. Anything seems possible.

July 23, 1944. I'm awakened just before dawn by a rumbling noise. Then an explosion and the entire prison shakes. The Americans are bombing again. Soon the air-raid siren starts up, followed quickly by the thud of antiaircraft fire.

I spend the morning staring out the window, hoping to catch a glimpse of an American plane. Just before noon I hear a commotion in the corridor. A few minutes later the water pipes tell the story:

All the guilty prisoners are being moved to this cell block. There could be only one reason—it will be easier to take us out for execution if we're all being held in the same area.

We're brought down to the trial room early in the afternoon. The general marches in with his aides, then stands at the long table without bothering to remove his hat or gloves. He unfolds a sheet of paper and begins to read aloud.

"I condemn to death . . ." He pauses, looking out at us, then proceeds to read a list of forty-seven names—all of the WIM prisoners except for the photographer and the two women.

Never before at Haaren have so many prisoners been sentenced to die in one trial. Even the guards stare in disbelief.

"Espionage is a very deadly enterprise," the general says. "All of you have taken a large part in it. Espionage is not protected by the Geneva Convention. It is my duty to condemn you to death."

We march back upstairs in stunned silence. It just doesn't make any sense. The Germans must know they can't get away with this. They're crazy to even try. The Allies will be here soon, and there will be investigations. They should be worrying about their own necks.

It's quiet in the cells. No one is even attempting to communicate on the pipeline.

Jan gazes at the floor, shaking his head. Even though he's in no danger, he seems as upset by the sentences as any of us. "They are up to something," I tell him. "I don't want to raise any false hopes, but they can't be serious about this. They must be hoping one of us will crack. And we can't let that happen. If need be, we must all go out to be shot without a whimper."

Chapter Ten

Night-and-Fog

July 24, 1944. After breakfast the guards come and move Jan to a new cell. "I shall pray for you," he says as they lead him away. He insists that I keep his New Testament.

I'm still not sure what the Germans hoped to accomplish by giving me a roommate. Not that it matters now that I'm alone again.

The grapevine is quite active today. More rumors, all of them contradictory. We're to be executed tonight. We're not to be executed at all. Another trial is to be held. There won't be another trial, but the one just finished will be reopened.

July 25, 1944. More bombing today. Still no indication when (or if) they plan to carry out the tribunal's sentence.

It's hard being alone again.

July 26, 1944. Still no word. Perhaps it's all a bluff. Perhaps they're just waiting for one of us to crack.

July 27, 1944. In the evening, after dinner, a guard comes in and blacks out my window. So the time has finally come. I feel strangely calm.

The guard leaves me a small scrap of paper and a stubby little pencil. For my last words, I suppose. What can I write? I don't

need a will, since I have no property to give away. I've hardly begun
to live my life, so there's no long story to tell. I don't even have a
future, so what good are my hopes and dreams?

I decide to write to my mother. I've got to phrase the letter carefully.
Anything too provocative and the Gestapo censors won't let it through.
At the same time I want to encourage her and Pa and Simone—to
let them know that if they can stick it out for a few more months,
everything will be all right.

"Dear Mother," I begin, "I do not know if this will ever reach
you. I hope it does because it should give you new hope. From the
little news we get occasionally I am sure it won't be very long anymore
before the war ends. I am fine and my morale is holding up very
well. Whatever happens, I want you to know how much I love all
three of you and that Pa should be proud of his son. I have tried to
live up to his expectations. Many kisses from your loving son."

I lie awake all night waiting for them to come for me.

July 28, 1944. A guard flings open my door shortly after dawn. He
tosses in a bundle of clothing, then quickly slams the door shut.
Are we to be executed in daylight?

As I dress, I hear a commotion outside. It sounds as if all the
prisoners in the block are being taken out of their cells. A few minutes
later the guard returns and leads me into the corridor. Sure enough,
all the other condemned agents are lined up along the wall. No
one has any idea what's going on.

After a few minutes we're marched downstairs to an interior courtyard. It is a pleasant, sunny day. The guards arrange us in rows
and order us to attention. We stand there in silence for perhaps an
hour. Finally, an officer comes out and murmurs something to the
sergeant who heads the guard detail. The sergeant shouts an order;
without any explanation, we're marched back upstairs to our cells.

Now the grapevine really comes alive, rumors flying like crazy.
According to the most persistent one, the Allies are closing in on
Haaren, and we are to be moved to another prison.

July 29, 1944. Hard to sleep—a combination of the uncertainty and
the continued Allied bombing.

We're roused at dawn and once again marched downstairs. This time, a convoy of trucks and jeeps with machine guns mounted on them is parked in the courtyard. So we are to be moved, after all.

Just like yesterday, the guards line us up in rows. Then they begin distributing small parcels containing our personal belongings. I peek into mine. Sure enough, there's the shirt I was wearing the day the Gestapo arrested me—the fine blue one that Charlotte gave me when we first met in Spain. It's torn and bloodstained, but otherwise clean and neatly folded.

As we're being loaded onto the trucks, I ask one of the guards where we're going. He looks around to make sure none of the officers is watching, then whispers, "Anrath." The name means nothing to me, except that it's German.

Anrath turns out to be not very far inside Germany—just thirty kilometers or so from the Dutch border. The journey there takes three or four hours. None of us can believe what the Allied bombing has done to the countryside. There is barely a house left standing anywhere. The sight of all this devastation does wonders for our morale—surely the war will end soon.

The prison at Anrath is an ugly place, all brick and stone. A troop of armed guards is waiting for us in the courtyard. We climb out of the trucks and stand there in silence, clutching the small bundles that contain our personal belongings. Finally, an officer comes out. He shouts some curses at us, then orders us to strip. When we're all naked, we're called up one by one and ordered to bend over so the guards can check to see if anyone has hidden anything up his bottom. Apparently, no one has. After that, the guards confiscate the parcels containing our personal belongings. In their place, we're each given a gray shirt, trousers, and a pair of wooden-soled shoes. All the shirts have the letters "N.N." stenciled on them.

Once we're dressed, they call the roll. For the first time I realize that not everyone in the WIM group has been sent to Anrath. Where could the others be? Surely they haven't been executed. No, that would be too crazy even for the Germans.

Finally, they march us to our cells. It seems that everyone is to be kept in solitary here. I'm used to being isolated, but the others aren't—I wonder how they'll take to suddenly finding themselves alone.

My cell is small—about two meters wide, maybe three meters long—with a stone floor. There's a metal table attached to one wall, an iron stool, and a small sink with one faucet.

July 30, 1944. According to the guards here, we are all dead men. They call us *"Nacht und Nebel Gefangene"*—"night-and-fog prisoners." That's what the "N.N." on our shirts stands for. So we don't forget the sentence hovering over us (as if any of us could!), those letters are branded everywhere: on the doors to our cells, even on the tin cups we've been issued.

July 31, 1944. Shortly after breakfast (two pieces of sticky bread), I'm taken from my cell and put in a line with a half dozen other prisoners, none of whom I recognize. We're marched across the courtyard to a large, warehouselike building. Inside is a wood shop. I'm put to work with another prisoner (a Yugoslav, I think) assembling wooden chairs with carpenter's glue.

What a wonderful change. It hardly matters that the Yugoslav and I don't speak the same language—it's great just to be in the same room with another person.

August 5, 1944. The chairs I'm making aren't very good, but who cares? I'm with other prisoners, and I've got something to do to keep busy.

The wood shop is a bit of a joke. For one thing, we keep running short of glue. The reason is that some of the prisoners are eating the stuff. I can't really blame them. The food here is horrible—much worse than it was at Haaren. Breakfast consists of two thin slices of very dark, sticky bread and a tin cup of coffee (at least that's what they call it). Lunch is a cup of cabbage soup. (So far it's contained actual cabbage leaves only once.) For dinner, we get another chunk of bread. Not surprising that my stomach is worse than ever.

August 8, 1944. For some reason, no one comes to take me to the wood shop. Instead, I'm left alone in my cell all morning. Lunch today is a cup of soup made from stinging nettles—with the roots left in.

I ask the prison trusty who brings the soup if the wood shop is closed today. Before he can answer, the guard in the hall shouts at me to be quiet and slams shut my cell door. Any and all communication with the night-and-fog prisoners is strictly forbidden.

August 9, 1944. Once again no wood shop. I think I know what has happened. Most likely, I was never supposed to have been sent there in the first place. Some poor clerk probably caught hell when they discovered that the infamous Raymond had been allowed to work in a shop with other prisoners.

August 11, 1944. Heard bombing in the distance last night. If the Allies have penetrated this far, the war must surely be drawing to an end.

After lunch I'm taken outside for fifteen minutes of "exercise"—a short walk in a small yard surrounded by barbed wire. No other prisoners in sight.

August 19, 1944. It was my birthday yesterday. I'm twenty-three now. Didn't remember it until this morning. Strange—a birthday's the last thing you'd think you'd forget.

It's amazing how much effort and energy a prisoner puts into keeping track of what time and day it is—and yet every once in a while there are mornings like this, when I wake up and can't remember what yesterday was. It's terrifying. Makes me wonder if I'm going crazy.

Then, again, maybe it's a good sign. I've been putting a lot of effort into trying to forget a lot of things, such as names, addresses, and faces—things I'd rather not be able to remember in case the torture ever gets unbearable.

They've been taking me out for my little walk every other day. I look forward to it enormously. The rest of the time I lie on my bunk, daydreaming. I've been trying to communicate with the other prisoners through the water pipe, but the grapevine here is nothing compared to what it was at Haaren.

August 26, 1944. Rumors are circulating that we're going to be executed sometime soon. How many times have I heard that one?

September 5, 1944. After breakfast, the guards pass the word that we're to prepare for transport. Transport? To where?

Shortly before noon we're taken from our cells and marched down to the courtyard. Good to see some non-German faces for a change (even if most of them are as gaunt as scarecrows). The guards distribute the parcels containing our personal belongings, then load us into a convoy of trucks.

We head east, through Düsseldorf. The city is a shambles, eighty percent of it bombed flat. Nothing to see but piles of rocky debris where houses used to be. Occasionally, a plume of smoke curls out from under the rubble—a sign that someone is living in the cellar.

I've never seen destruction on this scale. How can the Germans go on fighting with their cities devastated like this? It's crazy, impossible. The war is bound to end any day now. It has to. They just can't go on.

Just before dark we reach our destination—the Gestapo prison at Luttringhausen, a small town about thirty kilometers east of Düsseldorf. From the outside, the prison looks much like Anrath. Inside, however, it's different. For one thing, the cells have wooden floors.

When they open the door of what is to be my cell, I notice that the floor is surprisingly shiny. It's as if someone has been polishing it. That doesn't make any sense. Who would bother polishing the floor of a cell?

As the guard pushes me inside, he hands me a short wooden stick. It looks like part of a broom handle, three-quarters of an inch in diameter and about ten inches long. I stare at the thing, confused. Then the guard explains what it's for: I'm to use it to polish the floor.

"Isn't there a piece missing?" I ask him.

He shakes his head. I'm to keep the floor shiny by rubbing it with the end of the stick. Either that or I don't get fed.

September 12, 1944. Allied bombing almost every night since I've been here. Through my window I can occasionally hear other prisoners moving around in the courtyard. I wonder if I'm the only one being kept in solitary here.

The Allied bombing continued. Over the next two months Gaston grew used to it. He also became quite expert at polishing the floor with his stick.

October 15, 1944. Huge bombing raid last night. Must have been hundreds of British and American planes—Lancasters and Flying Fortresses, by the sound of them—laying down what they call a "carpet" of bombs, one next to the other, just a few miles from here.

It's a terrifying experience. First the walls start to vibrate, then the cells themselves begin to rattle. Finally, even the door hinges and the locks are vibrating. Hard to know which of my emotions is stronger: fear that one of the bombs will fall on top of my cell, or joy because all this shows how far the Allies have advanced.

October 25, 1944. I can hear a group of prisoners in the yard below my cell. It used to bother me that I was the only one being kept in solitary. Not anymore—at this point I don't think I'd really want to share my cell with anyone. I've come to the conclusion that solitude suits me.

November 19, 1944. Working on the floor this morning reminded me of killing the fleas at Fresnes. No fleas here. No records to set either, not in flea killing or floor polishing. I've got to conserve my strength. Liberation could come any day now.

My stomach is getting worse. Terrible cramps every time I eat.

November 20, 1944. Another carpet-bombing raid last night. Must be the steelworks just south of here at Remscheid and Solingen. We drove past them on our way from Anrath. How long ago that seems. It was warm then. Now it's cold and rainy.

November 23, 1944. Dreamt about my parents last night. What's become of them? Are they alive or dead? I must survive to find out.

December 8, 1944. Major bombing last night, quite close to here. For a while I thought the prison might be the target. That's crazy, of course. Surely, the Allies know we're here. They wouldn't bomb us. I feel quite sure of that.

December 15, 1944. My stomach ulcers are becoming increasingly unbearable. Every time I eat something, I get terrible pains for the first five or ten minutes. They go away for a half hour or so, then return worse than ever for as long as three hours.

I don't know how much longer I can go on like this. Perhaps it would be better if I didn't eat all my food at once, but spaced it out over a couple of hours.

December 20, 1944. A lot of snow outside. Word over the water pipes that there's been a very big Allied offensive in the Ardennes. That's only sixty or seventy kilometers from here. Maybe we'll all be free by Christmas. Wouldn't that be something?

December 25, 1944. My second Christmas in captivity. For breakfast, I get an extra slice of bread—*white* bread.

At lunchtime one of the Dutch trusties who helps serve the cabbage soup leans toward me and whispers, "Things are going very well." Then he straightens up and says loudly, "We have a nice Christmas tree down in the main hall." The guard shouts at him to shut up.

It gets dark quite early. Shortly after the sun goes down, I hear what sounds like a choir singing a Christmas carol. How peaceful and lovely. Then the air-raid sirens start to scream, and all the prison lights snap off.

A few minutes later the bombs start to fall. Sounds like they're hitting about ten or fifteen kilometers from here.

January 1, 1945. How is it possible that the war has lasted this long? What keeps the Germans going? Why aren't the Allies here yet? I have nothing but questions and no one to answer them.

January 8, 1945. My new eating regime doesn't seem to be helping me. It's ridiculous anyway—if my stomach can't handle two pieces of bread at once, why should spacing them out over three hours make any difference? Perhaps I should just try to eat less.

Gaston's health continued to deteriorate. Eating less helped alleviate his cramps, but it left him pitifully weak. He found it difficult to stand up after sitting or lying down for any length of time. Abrupt motion—no matter how insignificant—made his head swim. He learned to get around by using a slow, robotlike shuffle.

March 2, 1945. Word on the grapevine is that the Allies have driven the Germans out of Belgium. Can this be true? I know it is. It must be.

Our turn will come soon, I'm sure of it. They're bombing nearly every night now.

March 7, 1945. The guards seem very nervous. According to the grapevine, Allied troops have broken the Siegfried Line and are advancing fast. When will they be here?

March 12, 1945. The guards are very nervous. Our rations have been reduced. Sometimes they skip a meal entirely.

Word is the Allies have taken Cologne and crossed the Rhine. If that's true, they should be here in a matter of days. Maybe even tomorrow.

March 15, 1945. Our rations have been cut back even further. Not that it matters much to me. I can barely eat anything without terrible pain.

March 24, 1945. Wild talk on the grapevine that the Germans will execute all the night-and-fog prisoners rather than let the Allies liberate them. Nonsense. They wouldn't dare.

April 5, 1945. The pain in my belly is just awful—so bad that I worry that these months in prison may have done me some permanent damage. I've taken to lying on the floor of my cell to avoid the dizziness.

I wonder if I'll be able to resume my studies when the war ends. Or will I have to live like an invalid? Maybe I won't be able to father children. It probably wouldn't be fair to get married if I couldn't. I know children are very important to Raymonde. I suppose that comes from her being a Catholic.

I can't imagine what it would be like to see Raymonde now. What would she make of my new philosophy and outlook? I feel like I've aged twenty years since I saw her last.

I dreamt of home last night, of my room in Ghent. After all the fighting, I wonder if the house is still standing. And what of my parents and Simone? I hope they're all right. Do they know how much I love them?

April 17, 1945. They're bombing every day now, in daylight as well as at night, for at least three hours at a time. They say the Allies have invaded the Ruhr, and the Germans are falling back for a last stand around Berlin.

April 25, 1945. The sound of the bombing has changed. In the distance I think I can hear cannons. When I lie on the floor of my cell, I can hear some kind of a rolling noise—like a long, heavy train rumbling in the distance.

May 3, 1945. The fighting sounds like it's very close to here. There's an almost never-ending rumble. Sometimes I think I hear the shouts of the soldiers, but that can't be. I'm sure it's just my imagination.

May 6, 1945. There's a wild rumor going round that Hitler is dead. How can that be? They're still fighting out there.

May 7, 1945. The bombing seems worse than ever. Not many planes. Mostly cannons. The prison shakes continuously. I've stopped listening to the grapevine. The rumors are too crazy to follow.

May 8, 1945. I wake up early. Something's very wrong. For a long moment I can't put my finger on it. Then it dawns on me. The silence. Everything is completely silent—outside, inside, it's all the same. The rumble, the bombing, the slamming of cell doors, the yelling of the guards—they're all gone. All that's left is a silence so thick and heavy that it's almost hard to bear.

All of a sudden I realize that it was quiet last night, too. Why didn't I realize it then? I seem to recall hearing a lot of cells being opened very late. Or was it very early this morning? Or maybe I dreamt it. No, I clearly heard some cells being opened and the guards yelling and swearing in German like they always do. But I didn't hear the usual second slam when they relock the cells. What could have been going on? Am I finally cracking up?

I lie on my bunk for what seems like hours. Nothing—not a sound. Have I gone deaf? I snap my fingers to make sure my ears are all right.

Then, very faintly, I hear something. Somewhere in the distant reaches of the prison, it sounds as if a cell door is being opened. That's it—first the metallic echo of the bolt being flipped up, then the creak as the heavy lock bar is slid back, and the crash as it falls against the door. Then . . . nothing. No voices, no shouting, no slam as the door is relocked.

A few minutes later, the same sequence of sounds repeats itself. It's just like last night—doors are being opened without being closed again—except this time I don't hear the guards yelling in German.

The noises come closer. They will reach my cell soon. Then they recede. They must have been coming from the floor below me. Yes, that's right. I can hear them starting up again on this floor. They're coming closer now. There are footsteps coming down the corridor. I sit on my bunk staring at the peephole in my door. No one flips up the cover to look through. Instead, with no preliminary check by the guard, the door to my cell is flung open—*wide* open—and an American soldier wearing olive-green combat fatigues steps in. He must be as young as I am, but he looks at least eight feet tall. I try to get up, but I can't.

The soldier smiles at me. "Okay, boy," he says. "It's all over now."

I sit on my bed staring at him. What is he talking about? A moment later three other men come into my cell—two more American soldiers and a German civilian. The German nods at me politely and asks if I am Gaston Vandermeerssche. *Herr* Vandermeerssche, he calls me. I can hardly believe my ears. I'd forgotten that German could be spoken so softly and with such deference.

The German tells me that he is working for the American First Army, which has occupied the Ruhr together with some British units. They are compiling a list of all the POWs and are particularly interested in the status of the *Nacht und Nebel* prisoners. He smiles at me encouragingly.

My brain feels fuzzy. I don't know what to say to these men. Is it really all over?

One of the soldiers tosses a package on the bed next to me. "It's food," he says. I stare at it. "Don't worry," the soldier continues, "there's plenty more coming."

The words mean nothing to me. All I can think is one thing. It's over. The war is over. The war is over, and I have survived.

Epilogue

Gaston had survived—though not, as it turned out, by very much. The night before the Allies arrived, Gaston later learned, the commandant of Luttringhausen received orders from Berlin to take all the *Nacht und Nebel* prisoners and burn them to death with flamethrowers. Fortunately for Gaston and his fellow inmates, the commandant was well aware that units of the American First Army were only a few hours away. Fearful of Allied retaliation, and hoping a display of prudence might earn him the goodwill of those he assumed would be his new masters, the commandant decided to ignore Berlin's orders. Instead of killing his resistance prisoners, he executed eighty common criminals. The bodies of the ill-fated eighty were still smoldering when the first American GIs marched into Luttringhausen bright and early the next morning.

Though Gaston was eager—indeed, almost desperate—for news of his family, he was in no shape to do anything more than sleep for the better part of the next day. Finally, after a rudimentary debriefing by Allied intelligence officers, he was put on a train for Brussels, where he had arranged to stay overnight with Commandant Castiaux before going on home to Ghent.

After twenty-four months in prison, most of it in solitary confinement, Gaston found his first few hours back in the world disorienting, to say the least. To his intense astonishment (not to mention relief), he had prevailed—the war was over, and he was still alive. He had done his duty, served his country nobly, paying in the process all but the ultimate price. Yet no one in the throngs of travelers that swirled around him seemed the least bit interested. For nearly two years he had been dreaming about the day of liberation. Now it had come . . . and gone—an anticlimax of stunning proportions. Where, he wondered as he made his way through the Brussels train station, were the cheering crowds, the reception committees, the flowers, the kisses, the shouts of "Well done!" and "Welcome home!"?

He remembered having seen movies of liberation scenes at the end of the 1914–18 war. Weren't he and his fellow prisoners entitled to the same treatment? The world's apparent indifference made him question for the first time since that May afternoon in 1941 when he fled his home a step ahead of the Gestapo why he had done what he had done. Gaston thought he had acted out of a deeply felt sense of right and wrong. Certainly, he had not been looking for recognition. But if he hadn't, he wondered, why did he now feel so let down?

At Commandant Castiaux's house, Gaston learned that his mother and sister were both safe at home in Ghent. But his father's fate was still unknown. The elder Vandermeerssche had been arrested by the Gestapo in December 1943 and sent to the extermination camp at Mauthausen. Several thousand prisoners were believed to have been executed there in an orgy of killing that took place in the last few days before the Allies liberated the camp. Whether Joseph Vandermeerssche was among them was not immediately known.

After a tearful reunion with his mother and sister, Gaston returned to Brussels, where he had been instructed to report in at Army intelligence headquarters. There, to his surprise, he was given the uniform of a captain and his very own staff car, a huge brown Nash. When he joked to one of his fellow officers that he must be the youngest captain in the Belgian army, he was told with a straight face that he was.

Gaston's duties as an officer were considerable, and when he wasn't being treated for the stomach and duodenal ulcers he had developed during his years in prison, he spent most of his time pressing for news of his father. Finally, after a week or so, news arrived: His father had been found unconscious but still breathing among the bodies of the prisoners who had been massacred at Mauthausen. With no way of knowing who he was or where he was from, the Red Cross flew him to a hospital in Lille, where he lay in a coma for several days. It wasn't until he finally came to that the authorities were able to ascertain his identity.

Eighteen months at Mauthausen had left the old man so ill and emaciated that when he and his son were finally reunited at home in Ghent, Gaston, to his horror, did not at first recognize his father. Still, the reunion ended up a happy one. It turned out that one of Joseph Vandermeerssche's fellow prisoners at Mauthausen had been Gaston Garreyn, whose dairy shop in Brussels Gaston (in the guise of Raymond) had used as a letter box. From Garreyn, Joseph had learned something of his son's exploits, the knowledge of which helped to keep him alive. "I kept telling the others," the father said, "that I must survive because I have to see my son again."

In the weeks and months that followed, Gaston slowly began to readjust to normal life. With his family now safely back together again, his two main concerns became his education (after five years of war, he was deeply worried about his ability to resume his studies) and his health. Two years of intermittent torture and constant mental stress, plus the deficiencies of prison rations, had exacted a heavy toll, both physically and psychologically. After so long in solitary confinement, it wasn't until the end of 1945, when he was invited to lecture at a series of American colleges and universities, that Gaston found it possible to be comfortable in groups of more than three or four people. Worse, for years after his liberation, the merest mention of any wartime incident would bring on a bout of terrifying nightmares. And it would be nearly a decade before he could eat a normal diet again.

But perhaps the most difficult adjustment for Gaston to make involved the slowly dawning realization that, instead of having been a soldier in the cause of freedom, he may have been no more than a pawn in what he much later came to know as *Le Grand Jeu*—the Great Game.

To begin with, he was astonished by the number of people who, the war safely over, claimed to have been in the resistance. Even some whom he had known to be pro-Nazi during the first three years of the war were now calling themselves "war heroes." Worse, no one seemed to be challenging their claims. (In part, this is why Gaston refuses to this day to consider himself a hero. "The real heroes," he says, "almost all died during the war.")

At the same time, he was dismayed to learn that the mysterious "boys from London" were claiming to have no knowledge of his underground activities. If not for the fact that Gaston's old colleagues Marc and Aristide, along with some of his old network chiefs, ·like Sabot and Charlotte were around to vouch for his bona fides, London might well have denied entirely any knowledge of his existence.

Not surprisingly, Gaston became determined to find out what was going on. In particular, he wanted to know if this sudden and unexpected reticence to acknowledge his activities was somehow connected to the success with which the Nazis had been able to infiltrate the Dutch underground—if, in short, someone in London had a guilty conscience about the apparent ease with which German counterintelligence had been able to perpetrate its audacious and shockingly effective *Englandspiel*.

And so Gaston began asking questions, contacting former resistance leaders to see if they knew anything that could shed light on the murky situation. He didn't find out very much, but the little he did uncover was hardly reassuring. Why, for example, after Queen Wilhelmina had asked the Belgian government-in-exile to lend her people an agent who could "pick up the broken pieces" of the Dutch underground (a request that resulted in "Charlotte" tapping Gaston, who—under the nom de guerre of Rinus—founded the network known as WIM), were both the Dutch in London and their British overlords at the Special Operations Executive (SOE) unresponsive to the point of being actively hostile to WIM's efforts? Gaston was further disconcerted when he discovered the testimony of a prominent Dutch lawyer who worked in WIM for a few months and then escaped to London after the Gestapo began to infiltrate the organization. "When I arrived in London," the lawyer said, "I noticed that all the materials—microfilms, maps, drawings, etc.—that the WIM organization had sent to London . . . were gathering dust on some shelves."

Gaston wasn't sure what to make of any of this, but apparently he had struck a nerve somewhere, for in the summer of 1945 he received an anonymous telephone call warning him to drop his inquiries. "You did an outstanding job fighting for the Allied cause," the caller told him, "particularly for Belgium, Holland, and England. So don't spoil it now by asking too many questions. Remember, agents occasionally disappear in strange ways." Around the same time, all of SOE's files having to do with WIM and *Englandspiel*—and only those files—just happened to be destroyed in a mysterious fire that swept through the organization's London headquarters.

With few resources, nowhere to turn for help, and a life to get on with, Gaston found himself with no choice but to abandon his ad hoc investigation.

In the years since, Gaston completed his education, earning his long-sought doctorate in physics. He also wound up marrying Violette Castiaux, the daughter of his old friend and commander Albert Castiaux. After working for a number of multinational corporations, Gaston and Violette moved to the United States. They and their children settled in a suburb of Milwaukee, Wisconsin, where today Gaston heads a prosperous business highly specialized in the manufacture of abrasion testers for the graphic arts industry.

Over the years Gaston has thought a lot about the mystery surrounding SOE's handling of WIM and the Dutch underground. And while he has not arrived at any definite conclusions, he does have a number of interesting, informed speculations. For example, it is established historical fact that the upper echelons of the German military contained more than a few senior officers whose loyalty to Hitler and the Nazi party was less than complete. Among them was Admiral Canaris, the fabled director of the Abwehr, the German military's counterintelligence agency. Is it possible that, in an effort to improve Canaris's position—and thus enhance his chances of leading a military coup against Hitler—the British decided to make him look good by, in effect, feeding him the entire Dutch underground?

By the impersonal standards of *Le Grand Jeu*, the sacrifice of a few hundred (or even a few thousand) agents such as Gaston and his colleagues in WIM would be a small price to pay if it might lead to the Führer's overthrow. If this was the case, then all of WIM's efforts—and, by extension, everything Gaston did from the time Charlotte asked him to set up the organization—were no more than a meaningless charade.

It is possible that the answer to the question of what really happened lies in a dust-covered folder hidden among the British government's secret war archives. Unfortunately, those archives are sealed and will remain so until the year 2040. Gaston, for one, is thus unlikely ever to know for sure whether or not, despite all his efforts, his devotion, and his sacrifices, his wartime role was merely that of an unwitting pawn in Britain's "Great Game."

Afterword
by
Gaston Vandermeerssche

Shortly after my return from captivity in 1945, I was asked on several occasions to write or cooperate in the writing of a book about my wartime experiences. I turned down all these requests. There were two reasons for this. First, I didn't want to do a book about my experiences without knowing the answer to all my questions about what had really happened behind the scenes. Second, I wanted to get on with my life, to try as best as I could to make up for all the time I had lost during the war. In order to do this, I knew (just as the wallpaper in my childhood bedroom had instructed me) that I had to put the past behind me and look only forward.

It was only a few years ago that I finally changed my mind, after my friend Carl Moebius and his wife, Janet, convinced me that recording my experiences was not a matter of choice or decision but one of "finishing the job" that I had begun in 1940—in other words, it was an obligation I had.

My greatest hesitation and fear were—and still are—that in trying to fulfill this obligation I would be unjust toward those many wonderful men and women who gave all they had to defend the cause of freedom. Unjust because my memory might fail me, and for unknown or irrelevant reasons I might remember some agents better than others. Unjust also because I did not know, nor could I know, all the physical and mental tortures they had gone through. Physical suffering is

197

very hard to describe. Having gone through a lot of physical torture myself, I know that no words can adequately capture the emotion one experiences. God gave me the strength and the right circumstances so that, under interrogation, I managed not to reveal any names, locations, or other details that led to the arrest of any agent. But not everyone was so fortunate, and I cannot even start to imagine the psychological torment the unlucky ones went through afterward.

Much worse are cases like that of Willy Stienstra, one of my agents in southern Holland. Willy was able to get us much extremely valuable information directly from the Germans by pretending to be a Nazi sympathizer. But even though he had been imprisoned by the Gestapo and condemned to die along with the rest of us, he returned home after the war ended to find himself regarded with mistrust and suspicion. For a true patriot such as Willy, this was too much to take. After a long, losing battle, he finally took his own life.

The truth of dramas like this cannot really be described or understood.

My own "rehabilitation" after the war was a slow and painful process. Part of it was medical. For more than a year I could not eat any spices, onions, butter, or fatty foods. (Even ten years after the war, onions still would give me a stomachache.) Coffee was out; every time I had a cup, I would wind up being sick for several days.

Some of it was psychological. It took me several months to break myself of the habit of carefully picking up and eating every crumb of bread that I would find around my plate at the breakfast or dinner table. For years afterward any mention of a war story during the day would result in horrible nightmares for me that night. Once, dreaming of my fight with the Germans who arrested me in Perpignan, the nightmare became so intense that I kicked my wife, Violette, right out of our bed.

To overcome all this, to get back to a "normal" life, as I had decided to do, meant putting the war and my imprisonment behind me. So it is, I think, for many people who went through experiences similar to mine. This may be why most of the Gestapo prisoners who were fortunate enough to get home alive very seldom speak of their wartime experiences. When my children read the first draft of this book, it was all new to them. Similarly, when I went back to Europe in the spring of 1982 to retrace the steps of Raymond and Rinus with eighteen American friends, I discovered that the family of "Leopold," the aristocratic young man who replaced me as a courier in the Pyrenees (and, like me, was later arrested by the Gestapo and sent to a concentration camp), had never heard of any of his wartime exploits. "This is the first time my husband has ever talked of all this," his amazed wife told me.

In light of all this, I hope readers will appreciate the special meaning and value of the hundreds of hours spent by my wife, by Janet and Carl Moebius, and by our friend Carl Mueller, who sat down with me every Monday night for four and a half years and patiently and systematically helped me to call back into my memory what I had tried to push away forever. We were all constantly amazed how, little by little, details would come back to me. Out of these meetings came hundreds of pages of notes, which Allan Mayer combined with other research to produce this book.

At the very least, it is my hope that as a result of all these efforts some reader with similarly trying experiences in his past may find the courage to put the bad behind him and look forward in a positive and optimistic way.

In recent years, I have been asked a number of times what I think of patriotism and what seems to be the lack of it. My views on the subject may seem surprising. In the first place, I think it's quite normal for one to consider it an honor to be given the chance to sacrifice everything, including one's own life, for the sake of freedom. But having had the perhaps unusual opportunity to work closely not only with Belgian patriots but French, Dutch, and Luxembourger patriots as well, I have come to the conclusion that the kind of patriotism we have known in the past is no longer appropriate for the future. And I think that just as we have seen our notion of family relationships change, so too we will see the idea of patriotism change.

As far as I'm concerned, when it is limited to one nation, patriotism can lead to fanaticism. I feel that the fundamental basis of patriotism should be a belief in mankind and its freedom. The fact is, the values of mankind in general reach far beyond the aspirations of any one nation, any one religion, or any one geographical location. One must learn to discover the values and the similarities of human beings that go far beyond the color of their skin, the artificial and superficial

expressions of their creeds or religions, and especially beyond the
particular piece of land on which they live. The concept of "international patriotism" is the only guarantee, it seems to me, for lasting
world peace.

Acknowledgments

I would like to give special thanks to the following for each one's special help in the many tasks involved in the preparation of the material for this book: my brother-in-law, The Reverend René Castiaux; our old friends the family Desobry; my friend, Pierre de Stexhe (aka Léopold); my sister, Simone Vandermeerssche Galle; our daughter, Martine Vandermeerssche Giese; my Dutch agents, Mientje Proost Houtman and Léonie Overgoor van Rooy; Nancy Mueller; Gloria Panosh; Jovanka Ristic; my Dutch section chief, D.H. Schortinghuis; my friend and former boss, William Ugeux; my Dutch section chief, J.B. Vermeulen; Jamie Walters; and to our American friends, Anna Blum, Jo & Jim Brooksbank, Paul Craggs, Michael McCormick, Mary and John Emory, Mary and Reed Hinrichs, Anita Kramer, Janet and Carl Moebius, Mitzi and Jim Olson, Jamie Olson, Ruth Rickun, and Marie Wallau.

Above all, however, I wish to acknowledge my wife, Violette, who has contributed so very much to my total readjustment in life during the past forty years, and my children, Danièle, Martine, Lynn and Marc-Albert.

Gaston Vandermeerssche

Glossary

ABWEHR   German Counterespionage

ABWEHR 4   Giskes Counterespionage

AS   Armée Secrète (the French army of the Resistance)

BBC   British Broadcasting Corporation

BIP   Bureau d'Information et de Presse (The information agency of the united Resistance).

BI   Bureau Inlichtingen (Dutch Intelligence)

CNR   Conseil National de la Résistance (The French National Council of the Resistance).

CRAB   Centre de Recruitment de l'Armée Belge (Recruiting center of Belgian Army).

DST   Direction de la Surveillance du Territorie (French counterespionage and international security agency).

FFI   Forces Françaises de l'Intérieur, official name of Resistance movements in 1944.

GDN   Geheime Dienst Nederland (Dutch Secret Service).

GESTAPO   Geheime Staats Polizei (Nazi Secret Police).

I.D. (ID)   Inlichtingendienst (Dutch Intelligence).

MI–5   The British counterintelligence and security service (internal affairs).

MI–6   The British secret intelligence service (external affairs—military and economic).

MI–9	A section of the War Office responsible for creating escape routes in Europe.
O.D. (OD)	Ordedienst (Dutch Service).
OSS	Office of Strategic Services U.S. special operations.
S.D. (SD)	Sicherheitsdienst (German SS police).
SHAEFF	Supreme Headquarters Allied Expeditionary Forces (General Eisenhower's headquarters).
SI	Secret Intelligence (American intelligence agency).
SIS	Secret Intelligence Service (British intelligence agency).
SNCF	Société Nationale des Chemins de Fer (French National Railway).
SOE	Special Operation Executive. The secret British organization created in 1940 to raise, arm, fund, and train armies in German and Japanese occupied territories and nations allied to the Axis.
SS	Schutzstaffel The politico-military order of the Nazi Party by which Hitler ruled Germany and German-occupied territories.
ULTRA	Code name for intelligence derived from decrypting German Enigma-enciphered wireless traffic.

Bibliography

Aron, Robert. *Leopold III ou le Choix Impossible*. Paris: Plon, 1977.

Bailey, George. *Germans*. New York: Avon Books, Discus Books, 1972.

Bernard, Henri. *Histoire de la Résistance Européenne 39–45*. Paris: Marabout Université, 1968.

Blumenson, Martin. *The Vilde Affair*. Boston: Houghton Mifflin Co., 1977.

Cave Brown, Anthony. *Bodyguard of Lies*. New York: Harper & Row, 1975.

Cookridge, E. H. *Set Europe Ablaze*. New York: Thomas Y. Crowell Co., 1966.

De Jong, L. *Het Begin van het Englandspiel*. Gravenhage: Staatuitgevery's 1978.

———. *Het Illegale Werk*. Gravenhage: Staatuitgevery's, 1978.

De Neve, Edouard. *Glorieuzen*. Enschede: N. V. Voorheen Firma. Van der Loeff., 1946.

Dourlein, Pieter. *Inside North Pole*. London: William Kimber, 1953.

Dulles, Allen. *Great True Spy Stories*. New York: Ballantine Books, 1968.

Eisenhower, Dwight D. *Crusade in Europe*. Garden City, N.Y.: Garden City Books, 1948.

Eisner, Jack. *The Survivor.* New York: Bantam Books, 1980.

Fargo, Ladislas. *The Game of the Foxes.* New York: David McKay Co., 1972.

Foot, M. R. D. *S.O.E. in France.* London: Her Majesty's Stationery Office, 1966.

Forsyth, Frederick. *The Odessa File.* New York: Bantam Books, 1972.

Fourcade, Marie-Madeleine. *L'Arche de Nöe.* Vols. 1 and 2. Paris: Fayard, 1968.

————. *Noah's Ark: The Secret Underground.* London: Kensington Publishing Corp., Zebra Books, 1968.

Frankl, Viktor E. *Man's Search for Meaning.* Translated by Isle Lasch. Boston: Beacon Press, 1963.

Frenay, Henri. *The Night Will End.* Memoirs of a revolutionary translated from the French by Dan Hofstadter. New York: McGraw-Hill Book Co 1976.

Fuller, Jean Overton. *The German Penetration of S.O.E.* London: William Kimber, 1975.

Garnier, Raymond P. *The Tangled Web.* New York: Pantheon Books, 1968.

Giskes, H. J. *Londres Appelle Pôle Nord.* Paris: Librairie Plon, 1958.

Goodenough, Simon. *War Maps.* New York: St. Martin's Press, 1982.

Hallie, Philip. *Lest Innocent Blood Be Shed.* New York: Harper Colophon Books, 1980.

Hohne, Heinz. *Canaris.* Paris: Balland, 1976.

Lacaze, Andre. *Le Tunnel.* Paris: Julliard, 1978.

McPherson, Malcolm. *The Blood of His Servants.* New York: Times Books, 1984.

Miller, Russell. *The Resistance.* New York: Time-Life Books, 1979.

Montgomery, B. L. *The Memoirs of Field-Marshal Montgomery.* St James' Place, London: Collins, 1958.

Payne, Robert. *Adolph Hitler.* New York: Praeger Publishers, 1973.

Perrault, Gilles. *L'Orchestre Rouge.* Paris: Fayard, 1967.

Persico, Joseph E. *Piercing the Reich.* New York: Ballantine Books, 1979.

Rep, Jette. *Englandspiel.* Netherlands: Van Holkema & Warendorf Bussum, 1977.

Russell, Francis. *The Secret War.* New York: Time-Life Books, 1981.

Ryan, Cornelius. *A Bridge Too Far*. New York: Simon & Schuster Inc., Popular Library, 1974.

Schoenbrun, David. *Soldiers of the Night*. New York: New American Library, Meridian, 1980.

Stafford, David. *Britain and European Resistance 1940–1945*. Oxford: St. Anthony's College, 1980.

Stevenson, William. *A Man Called Intrepid*. New York: Ballantine Books, 1976.

Sykes, Christopher. *Tormented Loyalty*. New York: Harper & Row, 1969.

Ten Boom, Corrie. *The Hiding Place*. New York: Bantam Books, 1971.

Ugeux, William. *Le Passage de L'Iraty*. Lyon: Henneuse, 1962.

———. *Le °Groupe G' 1942–1944*. Paris/Brussels: Elsevier Sequoia, 1978.

Vening, Wil. *Verzetsgroep Zwaantje*. Naarden: Strengholt, 1978.

Young, Brigadier Peter. *World War II Almanac*. New York: World Almanac Publications, Bison, 1981.

Zu Lowenstein, Prince Hubertus. *What Was the German Resistance Movement?* Godesberg: Grafes, 1965.